Object Modeling &

Flow Diagramming

For Designers

Methods for designing with ease and confidence

◆◆◆ Heidi P. Adkisson

Object Modeling & Flow Diagramming for Designers
Methods for Designing with Ease and Confidence
By Heidi P. Adkisson

Companion website objectmodelingfordesigners.com

Editor: Ellen Nadelhoffer
Book Cover and Interior Design: Megan Greco
Proofreading: Pagetrim Book Services

Special thanks to test readers Geoff Harrison and Tristan Plank for their invaluable input and suggestions.

ISBN: 9798432160201

Table of Contents

Chapter 01

Introduction

In my 20-plus years of consulting work, I've addressed a wide range of design challenges, from relatively straightforward consumer apps to complex, highly specialized enterprise systems. Regardless of the design challenge, I've found it's essential to design from two points of view: the **structural perspective** and the **task perspective**.

As designers, the task perspective naturally demands our attention because, in the end, we are designing for people to accomplish tasks with a system. Task perspective artifacts include storyboards, journey maps, scenarios, and prototypes. But the structural perspective is equally important because it helps keep experiences simple and consistent across the range of tasks. Structural perspective artifacts include a system's overall architecture, system vocabulary, and global design conventions.

The ultimate goal is to marry together the task and structural perspectives to drive a better user experience.

This book covers two methods that help achieve that marriage:

- Object Modeling
- Task Flow Definition

Figure 1.1 summarizes how the structural and task perspectives work together in the overall design process.

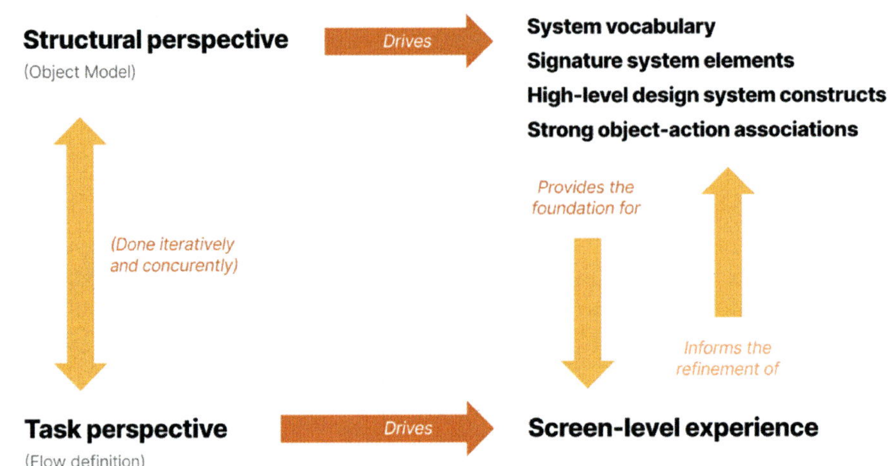

Figure 1.1
Designing from two perspectives (the structural perspective and the task perspective)

If you aren't familiar with object modeling, I think you'll find the process both insightful and useful. In addition to informing structural elements of the user experience, an object model abstracts a system from its current design, thus providing a fresh perspective.

In defining task flows, we'll look at methods to identify a system's primary flows and, importantly, its alternate flows (other success paths).

Who Should Read This Book?

If you are a UX professional designing applications, this book is for you! The methods described here apply to both consumer applications and enterprise systems targeted at business users. You'll find examples from both domains.

To get the most out of this book, you should have hands-on experience with user-centered design methods and be familiar with written system requirements, such as user stories. Because this book will take you step-by-step through the process of building object models and task flow diagrams, no other prerequisites are needed.

Why I Wrote this Book

The methods described in this book have helped me, over the years, design with greater ease and confidence. I've worked hard to refine these methods to share them more easily with others. When teaching object modeling in particular, I've found people excited about using the approach in their design practice.

This book allows me to share my ideas more broadly and describe the techniques in more detail than is possible in a workshop setting. I've greatly enjoyed writing the book, and in the process, thinking of you, my audience, and how you might engage with its contents.

About Me

I've been in the tech field since 1988 when I was one of the first employees in a (pre-web) start-up that provided software to wireless service providers. There, I had the opportunity to work closely with software developers and eventually transition into a role overseeing the company's operations. In 1997, I completed my MBA degree at the University of Washington.

However, by the late 1990s, it was increasingly apparent that my heart lay with design, and I was particularly interested in the then-nascent field of web design. A career transition and another degree later (MS in Human-Centered Design and Engineering), and I began my design career full-time in early 2001.

In making the transition to design, I was fortunate to land at Blink UX, a Seattle-based research and design firm. As a Design Principal at Blink, I've had the opportunity to work across an extensive range of project types for both consumers and the enterprise. Clients have included Apple, NASA, John Deere, Moen, AWS, Google, Microsoft, GE Power, First American Title, and JB Hunt.

What Will You Learn?

In this book, you will learn to work with source material, such as user stories and a system's existing interface, to create an object model that provides a compact representation of the system from the structural perspective. Figure 1.2 shows an example model for an e-commerce system.

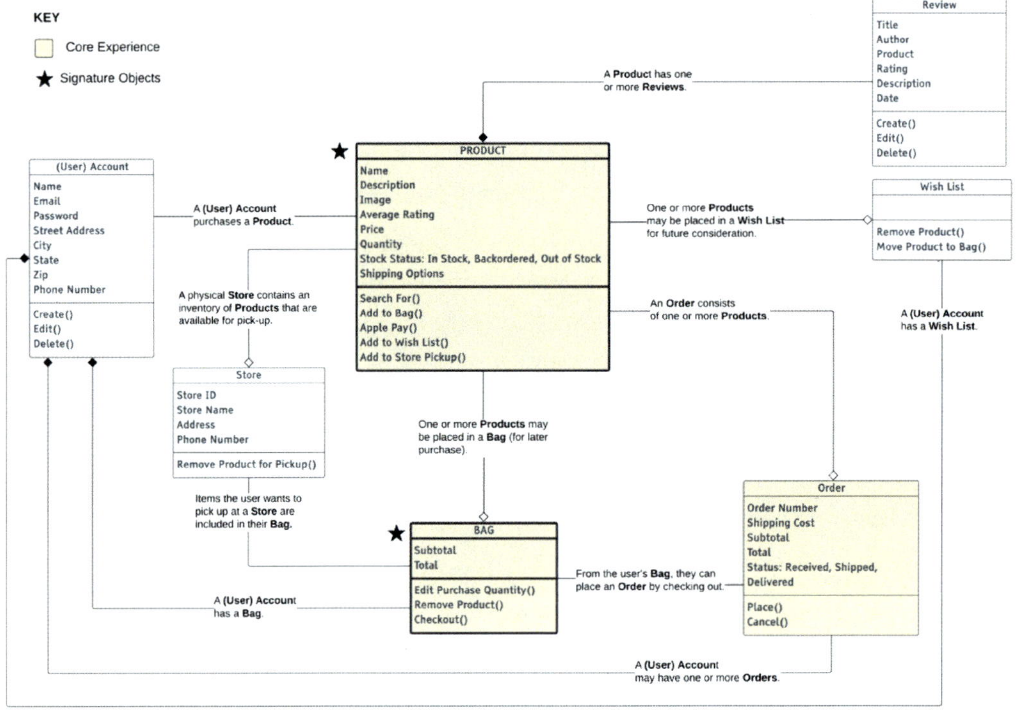

Figure 1.2
Object model for an e-commerce system

You'll learn to use the object model to represent a system's vocabulary, identify its signature elements, create higher-level design system constructs, and inform screen-level design.

You'll also learn everything you need to define effective task flows using standard flow-charting symbols, making your diagrams easier for others to read and understand (Figure 1.3). Additionally, this book shows you how to define flows using narrative, an approach that's particularly helpful in designing more complex flows.

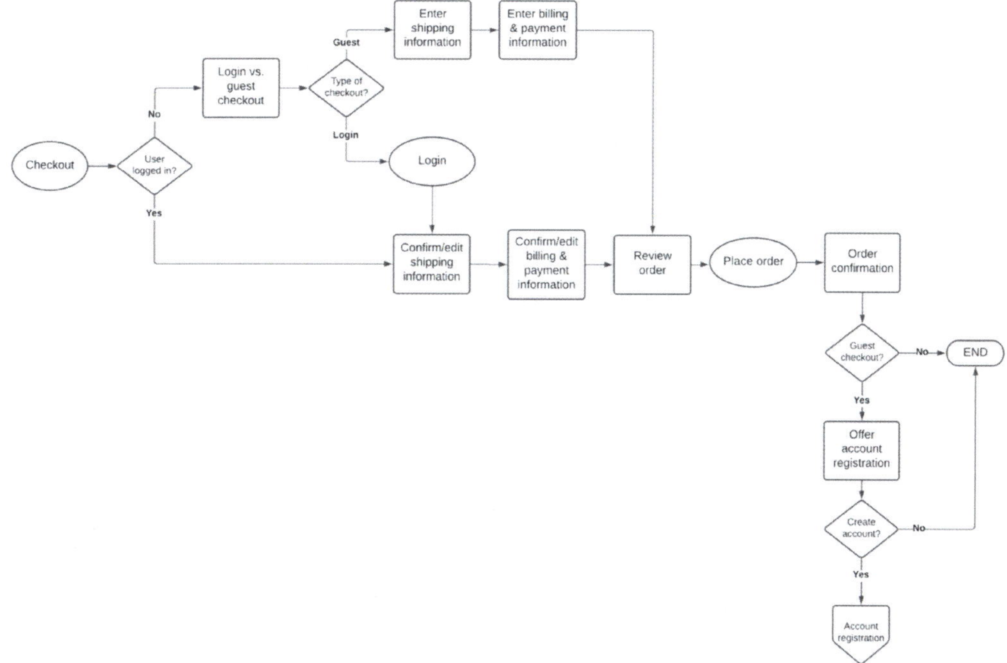

Figure 1.3
Task flow diagram for e-commerce checkout

Finally, you will learn how to integrate structural elements and task flows into an effective screen-level design, as summarized in Figure 1.1.

Additional Resources

I've done my best to format the many diagrams and illustrations in this book to be readable across the range of reading devices. You can also view any of the diagrams at objectmodelingfordesigners.com/book

Additionally, quick reference cards are available for both object modeling and task flow diagramming. You can download these at objectmodelingfordesigners.com/resources

Let's get started!

"The ultimate goal is to marry together the task and structural perspectives to drive a better user experience."

Objects

As a designer, you're probably already familiar with the idea of objects, though you may not think about them as such. For example, typical objects in an e-commerce system include *Product*, *Bag*, *Wish List*, and *Review*.

Each object has a set of associated actions. As shown in Figure 2.1, actions for the *Product* object might include *Search For, Add to Bag, Apple Pay, Add to Wish List, Add to Store Pickup*.

Product

Search For()
Add to Bag()
Apple Pay()
Add to Wish List()
Add to Store Pickup()

Figure 2.1
The *Product* object with associated actions

Thus, a system can be characterized (and modeled) according to its objects and actions.

A Short History of Objects and Actions

The centrality of objects and actions in modern systems stems from the development, in the mid-1970s, of the graphical user interface (GUI). The GUI is such a part of our lives today that it's easy to forget what a user experience revolution it was at the time. Before the GUI, users had to master either a command-line interface or, more challenging yet, punch cards (Figure 2.2).

Figure 2.2
Computer punch card operator in the 1960s

Thankfully, punch cards have been relegated to the history bin. However, the command-line interface (CLI) lives on and does have its advantages for some types of computing tasks. Even if you've never used a CLI, you might be familiar with it as the Windows command prompt or the macOS terminal (Figure 2.3).

```
john — -bash — 80×24
Last login: Wed Jun  2 09:29:22 on console

The default interactive shell is now zsh.
To update your account to use zsh, please run `chsh -s /bin/zsh`.
For more details, please visit https://support.apple.com/kb/HT208050.
johns-air:~ john$ sudo softwareupdate -l
Password:
Software Update Tool

Finding available software
Software Update found the following new or updated software:
* Label: macOS Big Sur 11.4-20F71
        Title: macOS Big Sur 11.4, Version: 11.4, Size: 11206447K, Recommended:
YES, Action: restart,
johns-air:~ john$
```

Figure 2.3
Example command-line interface

The command line can be a highly efficient method of interacting with a computer. However, there is a steep learning curve: users must type commands exactly and, to work efficiently, memorize commands. With the advent of the GUI, computing became wholly more accessible, requiring much less specialized knowledge.

The Xerox Star system (Figure 2.4), released in 1981, was the first commercially available system with a GUI. It inspired other early GUI-based computers, including the Apple Lisa (in 1983) and the Apple Macintosh (in 1984).

Figure 2.4
The Xerox Star system (1981)

Modeling Objects

Today objects and actions are foundational to any user experience. As we'll see in the chapters that follow, **modeling a system's objects** can help streamline the design process and improve design outcomes.

Readers familiar with the Unified Modeling Language (UML) will recognize that the practice of modeling objects is not new. UML is a notational system created in the 1990s to represent system design using a standard set of diagrams. In 1994, Rational Software developed UML as part of its suite of developer tools. Since then, the International Organization for Standardization (ISO) has managed UML as a standard. There are two main types of UML models: **behavioral** and **structural**. As a designer, you might be familiar with a use case model, a behavioral model that represents tasks supported by a system. Figure 2.5 is an example of a use case model for a banking system.

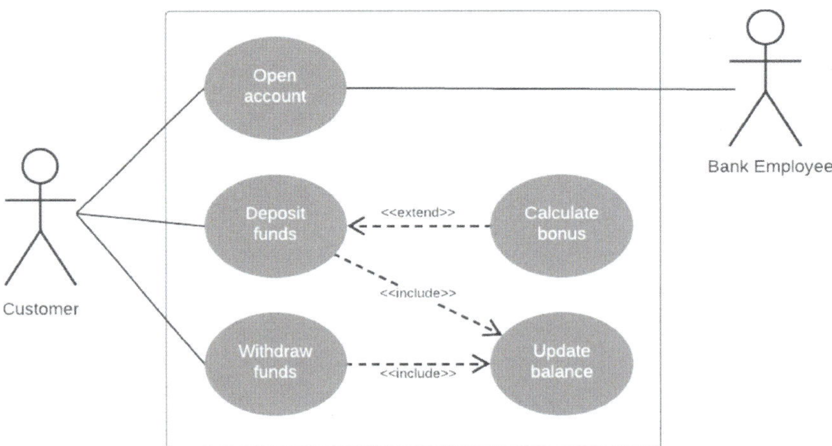

Figure 2.5
Use case model for a banking system

To understand object modeling, we will focus on a structural model: the **UML class diagram.** The class diagram illustrates a system's objects and the relationships between them.

Figure 2.6 is a simplified UML class diagram that illustrates the conventions:

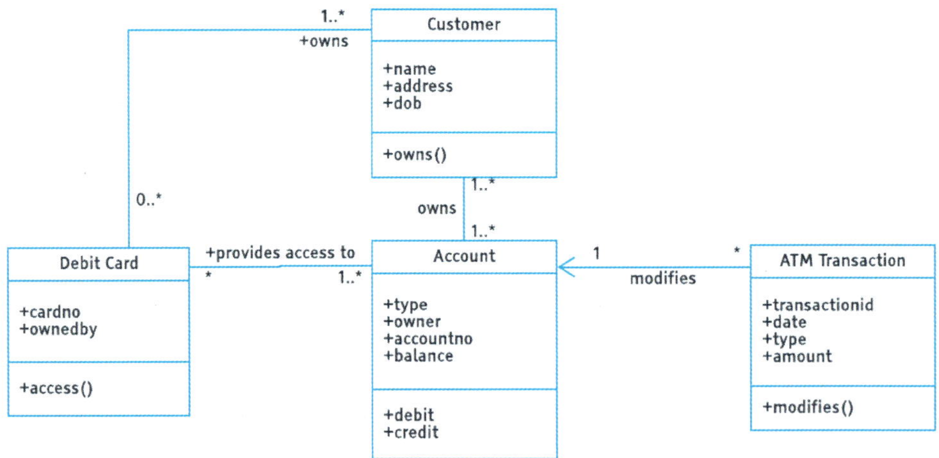

Figure 2.6
Simplified UML class diagram for an ATM. You can also view this diagram at
objectmodelingfordesigners.com/chapter-2

- The top pane of the object rectangle contains the name of the object.
- The lower pane displays each object's associated actions.
- The middle pane lists the object's attributes (associated data fields).
- Lines between the objects indicate relationships.

While the class diagram may be less familiar to designers today, its original intent was to serve as the basis of object-oriented user interface design. In fact, in the late 1990s and early 2000s, entire books were written on this topic (Figure 2.7).

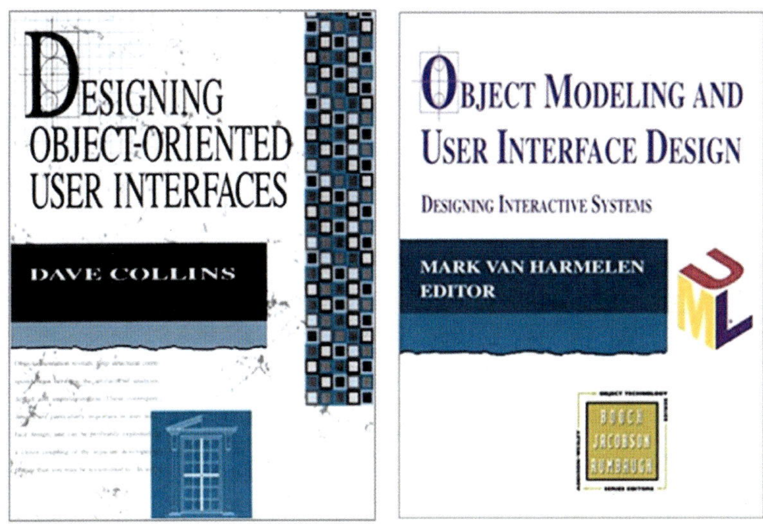

Figure 2.7
Books on object-oriented interface design

The Narrative Object Model

Creating a complete UML class diagram can be time-consuming and requires a set of skills more typical of an engineer or analyst. It's not something that a UX professional today would likely prepare. We can, however, take inspiration from the traditional UML class diagram and create a simpler, more accessible version—what I call a **narrative object model.** A narrative object model (mostly) dispenses with the UML notation and instead relies on a plain-English narrative.

Figure 2.8 is the ATM class diagram example (Figure 2.6) recreated as a narrative object model.

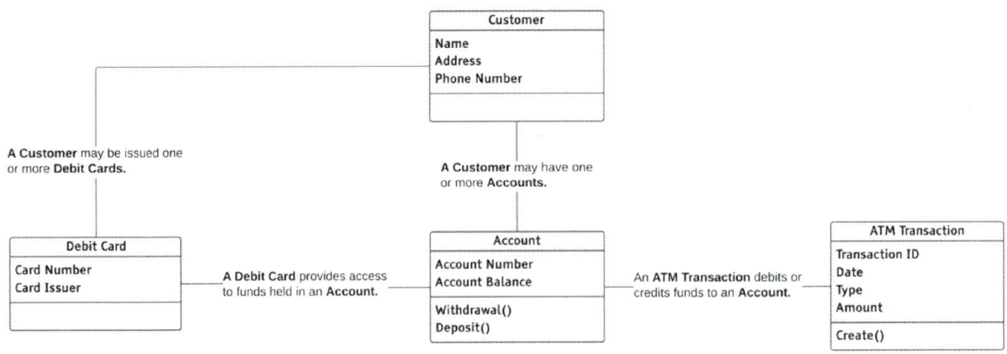

Figure 2.8
Narrative object model for an ATM. You can also view this diagram at objectmodelingfordesigners.com/chapter-2

In the chapters that follow, we'll walk through the process of creating a narrative object model, breaking the process into three main steps:

1) Identifying objects
2) Characterizing the relationships between objects
3) Identifying each object's actions and attributes

I advocate keeping your approach to object modeling flexible: to create the model that best serves your design needs. For example, building a complete model might not always make sense; sometimes, even just identifying the objects is enough. Later chapters contain examples of simplifying the modeling approach for different design circumstances.

Tools You'll Need

You can use any drawing program to create an object model; however, it should support dynamic connectors. It's ideal to have a palette with the standard line treatments for UML class diagrams since we are re-purposing some of those conventions. The models you see in this book were built using Lucidchart, but any similar application will do.

Building an initial model can also be done collaboratively as a team activity. To do this in person, all you need is a set of sticky notes and a whiteboard or a large expanse of paper (such as butcher paper). Virtually, you can use a collaborative working space such as Mural. For more on creating models collaboratively, see objectmodelingfordesigners.com/resources

Starting Points and Project Types

Creating any object model begins with identifying its objects. Depending on your design project type, you'll likely have a mix of resources to use as your starting point. This book will walk you through how to use two primary sources:

- User stories (or similar requirements documentation)
- A system's existing interface

The mix of sources you will rely upon depends on the type of design project at hand, as summarized in Figure 2.9.

Type of project	Existing interface	Requirements documentation
Greenfield design		◆
Redesign/ re-platforming	◆	◆
Feature release	◆	◆

Figure 2.9
Types of design projects and sources for object modeling

Greenfield design is designing a new application or system from the ground up; there is no existing starting point, and you are building the experience from scratch. In this case, you are likely only working from user stories or other types of requirements resources. Following a Lean methodology, the initial release in a greenfield design project may be a Minimal Viable Product (MVP).

In the purest sense, a **redesign** takes an existing system and redesigns it to improve the user experience. This type of redesign commonly occurs with legacy systems and may also involve re-platforming (for example, moving it from a desktop client to the browser). In this case, you may be creating the model primarily or even exclusively by inspecting the current interface without user stories to reference.

A **feature release** is adding new features to an existing system. In this case, I advocate modeling the new features as part of modeling the system as a whole, referencing both the current interface and the requirements documentation for the new features. This approach helps ensure the new features are appropriately architected into the overall experience.

Identifying Objects

The easiest way to think about objects is that they are the nouns in a system (rather than the verbs, which represent actions). Each object is represented by a rectangle in the model, as shown in Figure 2.10.

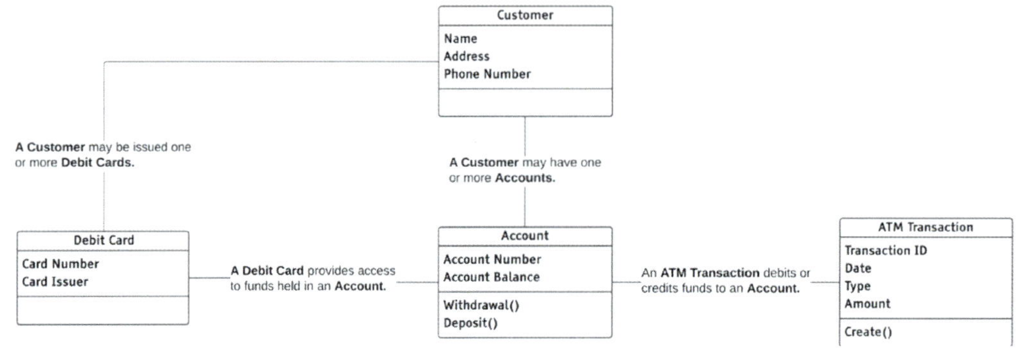

Figure 2.10
Narrative object model for an ATM. You can also view this diagram at objectmodelingfordesigners.com/chapter-2

It's important to understand the difference between an object, which represents a concept, and an instance of an object. In Figure 2.11, *Customer* is the object, and the instances of that object are the specific database records for Jose E. Hamill, Jamie Averett, and Tiffany Scott.

Object

Customer
Name
Address
Phone Number

Instances

Jose E. Hamill
4310 Ben Street
Sedalia, MO 65302
518-269-9354

Jamie Averett
2446 Taylor Street
New York, NY 10013
914-598-6717

Tiffany Scott
934 Goodwin Avenue
Omak, WA 98841
509-429-4885

Figure 2.11
The *Customer* object and example instances of that object

To identify objects, we'll use two different resources:

- An existing interface
- User stories

Identifying Objects from an Existing Interface

By first walking through how to identify objects from an existing interface, we'll see examples of how objects are represented in a design. Menus and button bars typically provide fruitful "hunting grounds" for objects.

Figure 2.12 shows a tweet from Twitter.com. It has a contextual menu at the top (A), a button bar at the bottom (B), and another contextual menu at the bottom (C). We'll use these elements to identify some nouns (objects).

Figure 2.12
Button bar and menus for a tweet

Figure 2.13 is the top contextual menu for a tweet with nouns highlighted.

Figure 2.13
Nouns highlighted in the contextual menu for a tweet

One object is *Account*, represented by the account name NASA (NASA being an instance of an account). *Tweet* and *List* are also objects. Figure 2.14 illustrates the objects.

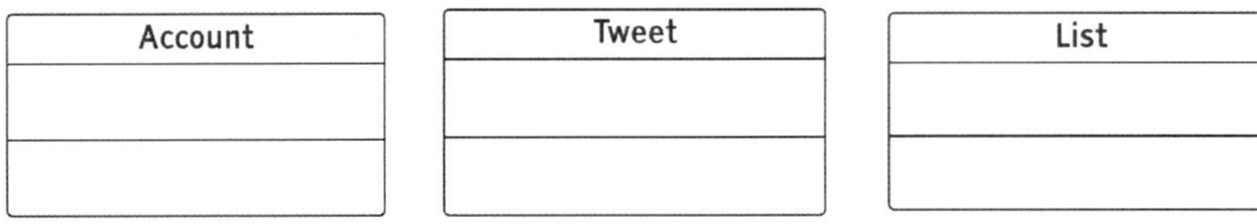

Account

Tweet

List

Figure 2.14
Objects from Twitter

The lower button bar contains options represented by unlabeled icons. Figure 2.15 shows the icons and their associated labels so that we can identify any additional objects.

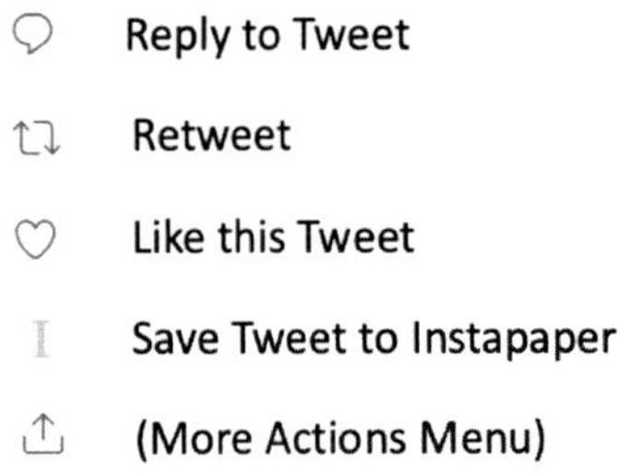

Reply to Tweet

Retweet

Like this Tweet

Save Tweet to Instapaper

(More Actions Menu)

Figure 2.15
Options represented in the button bar for a tweet

In this case, the icons represent actions that users can take against a tweet—an object we've already identified.

The last icon in the button bar, which looks like a share menu, is actually a "more actions" menu. Figure 2.16 shows this menu with its nouns highlighted.

Figure 2.16
Nouns highlighted in the contextual menu for a tweet

The "more actions" menu shows the *Tweet* object again, plus two new objects: *Direct Message* and *Bookmarks*. Figure 2.17 shows the consolidated list of Twitter objects we've identified so far.

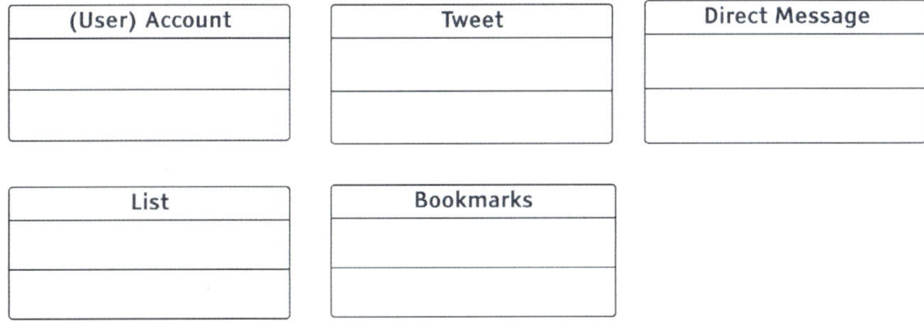

Figure 2.17
Objects identified for Twitter

Note that I renamed the Account object *(User) Account.* I did this to indicate the type of account (versus, for example, an administrator account). Additionally, as we'll see once we define relationships, the *(User) Account* label makes the model a bit easier to read.

Next, let's look at a different example from an e-commerce system. Figure 2.18 is a product detail page with its objects highlighted.

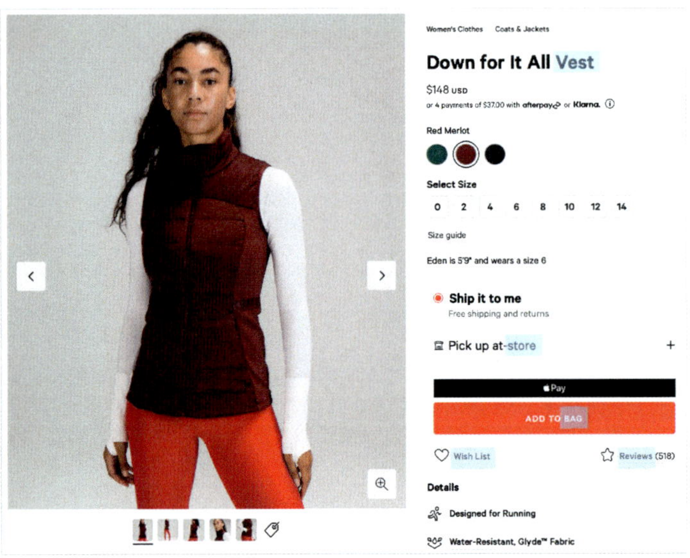

Figure 2.18
Product detail page with its objects highlighted

As shown in Figure 2.19, the objects we identified on the above product detail page are *Product*, *Store*, *Bag*, *Wish List* and *Review*.

Figure 2.19
Objects identified on the product detail page

In looking at the product detail page, you might wonder how to treat color and size. In this case, color and size are **attributes** of a *Product*, not objects in and of themselves, as is the case with the size guide and details content. Additionally, the photo of the product is not an object; it represents the *Image* attribute of a *Product*. Attributes are covered in a later chapter but think of them as data fields that would be part of a database record for an object.

Identifying Objects from User Stories

Another way to identify objects is using requirements documentation. We are going to focus on user stories, given their widespread use.

User stories should be familiar to designers who work in Agile development environments. They are short, simple expressions of system requirements told from the user's perspective and follow a standardized syntax as shown below:

> Syntax: As a <type of user>, I want <some goal> so that <some reason>.
> Example: As an unregistered user, I want to create an account so that I use the service.

We can use the goal statement part of a user story, which begins with "I want..." to identify objects. This statement expresses what action the user wants to take, and what objects are involved. The example below shows the goal statement in bold text.

> Syntax: As a <type of user>, **I want <some goal>** so that <some reason>.
> Example: As an unregistered user, **I want to create an account** so that I can use the service.

Here are some additional goal statements highlighted in a set of sample user stories for Twitter:

- As an unregistered user, **I want to create an account** so that I can use the service.
- As a user, **I want to send a tweet** so that I can communicate to my followers.
- As a user, **I want to add a hashtag to a tweet** so that my tweet can be grouped with other tweets that share the same hashtag.
- As a user, **I want to follow another person's account** so that I can see the tweets that they post.
- As a user, **I want to see tweets from all accounts I follow in a timeline** so they are all together in a single view.
- As a user, **I want to create a list of specific accounts** so that tweets from those accounts are together in a single view.
- As a user, **I want to add a tweet to my bookmarks** so I can easily refer to it later.
- As a user, **I want to send a direct message to another person's account** so

that I can communicate with them privately rather than publicly.

- As a user, **I want to see a list of trending hashtags** so that I can stay up-to-date on the hottest topics.

To identify the objects, we can highlight all the nouns within each goal statement as shown below:

- As an unregistered user, **I want to create an account** so that I can use the service.
- As a user, **I want to send a tweet** so that I can communicate to my followers.
- As a user, **I want to add a hashtag to a tweet** so that my tweet can be grouped with other tweets that share the same hashtag.
- As a user, **I want to follow another person's account** so that I can see the tweets that they post.
- As a user, **I want to see tweets from all accounts I follow in a timeline** so they are all together in a single view.
- As a user, **I want to create a list of specific accounts** so that tweets from those accounts are together in a single view.
- As a user, **I want to add a tweet to my bookmarks** so I can easily refer to it later.
- As a user, **I want to send a direct message to another person's account** so that I can communicate with them privately rather than publicly.
- As a user, **I want to see a list of trending hashtags** so that I can stay up-to-date on the hottest topics.

Figure 2.20 shows the Twitter objects identified from the user stories above.

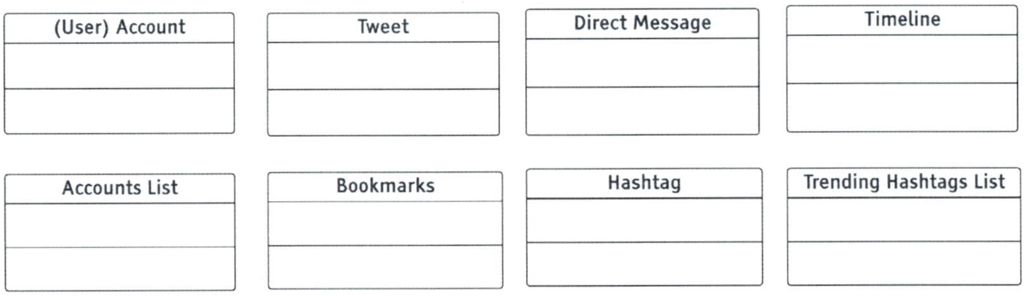

(User) Account	Tweet	Direct Message	Timeline

Accounts List	Bookmarks	Hashtag	Trending Hashtags List

Figure 2.20
Objects identified from the Twitter user stories

Here's another set of example user stories with their objects highlighted; this set is from an e-commerce system:

- As a user, **I want to search for products** so that I can find products that meet my needs.
- As a user, **I want to read reviews** so I can learn what other people think about the product.
- As a user, **I want to add products to my wish list** so that I can save items that I don't want to purchase now but might want to later.
- As a user, **I want to add products to my bag** so I can purchase them when I'm done shopping.
- As a user, **I want to pick up products I purchase at a nearby store** so that I can receive them more quickly.
- As a user, **I want to submit an order for products in my bag** so that I can receive them.
- As a user, **I want to create an account** so that I can have access to my order information and purchase history.
- As a user, **I want to review my orders** so that I can see what I've purchased in the past.
- As a user, **I want to create a review about the product I purchased** so that I can share my opinion with potential buyers.

Figure 2.21 shows the objects identified from the e-commerce user stories.

Figure 2.21
Objects identified in the e-commerce user stories

Identifying Objects as a Team

Identifying objects can be a team activity, either using a "divide and conquer" strategy or working all together from the same set of sources. As you identify objects, write each one on a sticky note, either a physical sticky note or in an online collaborative workspace. Group the duplicate sticky notes to create a consolidated list. Identifying objects as a team has the advantage of getting everyone involved in the process and creating a shared understanding of the objects.

Figure 2.22
Identifying objects as a team

Exercise A: Identifying Objects

Now it's your turn! For this exercise, you'll use a set of user stories for the online collaboration application Slack. (Don't worry if you're not familiar with Slack, you'll still be able to do this exercise.) Using the stories below, you'll do three things:

1) Identify the goal statements.
2) Highlight the nouns within each goal statement.
3) Create a list of objects.

The solution is in the next section.

a) As an administrator, I want to sign up for an account so that we can use the service for our organization.
b) As an administrator, I want to create one or more workspaces for my organization so that we will have our own dedicated space on Slack.
c) As an administrator, I want to invite users to join a workspace so that they can communicate together.
d) As an administrator, I want to create a channel so that posts on a particular topic can be kept all together within the channel.
e) As a user, I want to create an account so that I can use the Slack service.
f) As a user, I want to join a workspace so that I can communicate with others in that workspace.
g) As a user, I want to create posts in a channel so that I can communicate with others in that channel.
h) As a user, I want to send a direct message to another user so that we can communicate privately.
i) As a user, I want to edit a post or direct message I've already published so that I can correct any mistakes.
j) As a user, I want to delete a post or direct message so that people don't see posts that I've changed my mind about publishing.
k) As a user, I want to attach a file to a post or direct message so that I can share it with others.
l) As a user, I want to add a reaction to a post or direct message so that I can quickly show a response without having to type out a message
m) As a user, I want to initiate a call to another user so we can quickly talk in real-time.

Exercise A: Solution

In Exercise A, you identified the goal statements and nouns in a sample set of user stories for Slack. You then used the nouns you identified to create a consolidated list of objects. Here is the solution:

a) As an administrator, **I want to sign up for an account** so that we can use the service for our organization.
b) As an administrator, **I want to create one or more workspaces for my organization** so that we will have our own dedicated space on Slack.
c) As an administrator, **I want to invite users to join a workspace** so that they can communicate together.
d) As an administrator, **I want to create a channel** so that posts on a particular topic can be kept all together within the channel.
e) As a user, **I want to create an account** so that I can use the Slack service.
f) As a user, **I want to join a workspace** so that I can communicate with others in that workspace.
g) As a user, **I want to publish posts in a channel** so that I can communicate with others in that channel.
h) As a user, **I want to send a direct message to another user** so that we can communicate privately.
i) As a user, **I want to edit a post or direct message** I've already published so that I can correct any mistakes.
j) As a user, **I want to delete a post or direct message** so that people don't see posts that I've changed my mind about publishing.
k) As a user, **I want to attach a file to a post or direct message** so that I can share it with others.
l) As a user, **I want to add a reaction to a post or direct message** so that I can quickly show a response without having to type out a message.
m) As a user, I **want to initiate a call to another user** so we can quickly talk in real-time.

Figure 2.23 shows the identified objects for Exercise A.

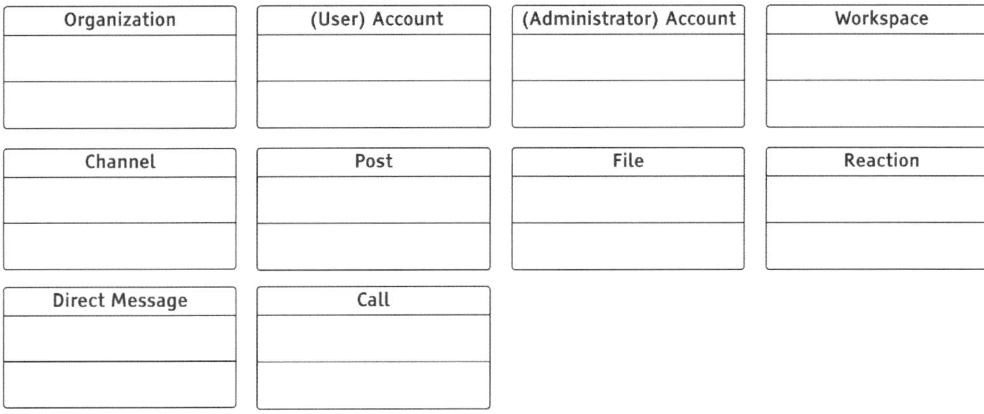

Organization
(User) Account
(Administrator) Account
Workspace
Channel
Post
File
Reaction
Direct Message
Call

Figure 2.23
Objects identified in the user stories for Slack

About the Solution

Note the special treatment of the account objects *(User) Account* and *(Administrator) Account*. As we'll see when defining relationships, indicating the type of account helps with the readability of the model.

Note also that I might have created a single *Account* object. However, I know from experience that different types of accounts generally have unique characteristics that I will want to represent in the model (thus, the two separate objects).

"The easiest way to think about objects is that they are the nouns in a system (rather than the verbs, which represent actions)."

Chapter 03

Object Relationships

With objects identified, we can begin building **relationships** between the objects. Relationships tell the structural story of the system, illustrating which objects are closely related and which have little or no relationship with one another. You can also consider objects and their relationships as a type of system ecosystem diagram, communicating, in a compact manner, the breadth of what the system entails.

Looking again at a traditional UML class diagram (Figure 3.1), we see that it uses specific notational conventions (indicated on the lines between objects) to show relationships.

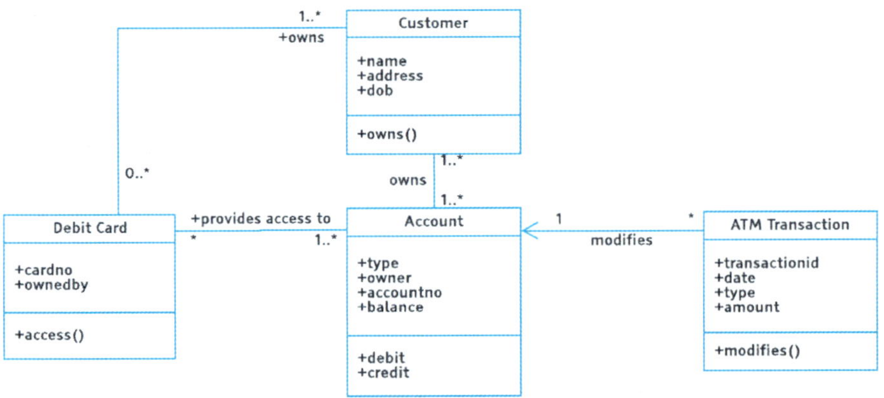

Figure 3.1
UML class diagram for an ATM. You can also view this diagram at
objectmodelingfordesigners.com/chapter-3

In creating a narrative object model, we will (mostly) dispense with the above notational conventions. Instead, we'll rely on plain-English narrative to describe the relationships between objects, as shown in Figure 3.2.

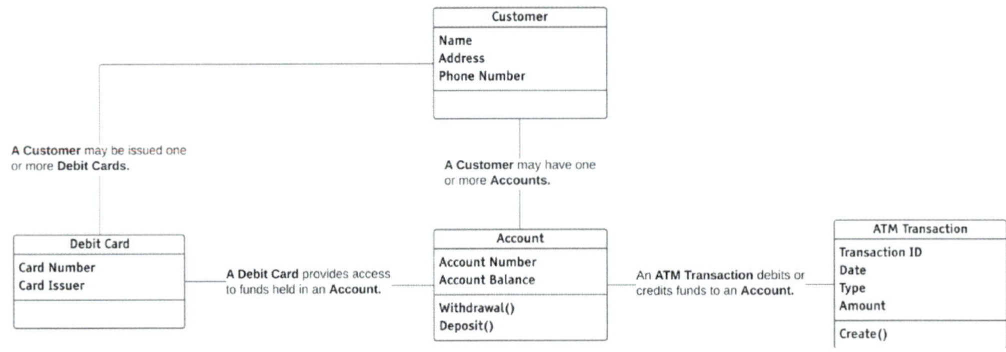

Figure 3.2
Narrative object model for an ATM. You can also view this diagram at
objectmodelingfordesigners.com/chapter-3

The figure above uses the following syntax for the relationship statements between objects:

<object> <verb phrase> <object>

The example relationship statements below show the syntax in action and use bold text to help the objects stand out within the statement:

- A **Customer** may be issued one or more **Debit Cards**.
- A **Customer** may have one or more **Accounts**.
- A **Debit Card** provides access to funds held in an **Account**.
- An **ATM Transaction** debits or credits funds to an **Account**.

Relationship statements are an essential part of the model. They should be written so that anyone reading the model can clearly understand them. Within the recommended syntax, there is flexibility to provide an additional explanatory narrative, as you'll see in some of the examples that follow.

The idea of identifying relationships may seem daunting at first. But in my experience, many people find defining relationships interesting and illuminating, and like anything else, it's easier if you take it step-by-step.

Types of Relationships

Using line treatments to indicate relationship types is a convention of a UML class diagram that I find helpful to carry forward into the simplified, more narrative object model. Though I consider line treatments optional (the relationship statements should carry the freight), indicating the relationship type can make using the model to inform design easier.

In a traditional UML class diagram, there are four main types of relationships:

- Association
- Aggregation
- Component
- Inheritance

These relationship types have corresponding line treatments, as shown in Figure 3.3.

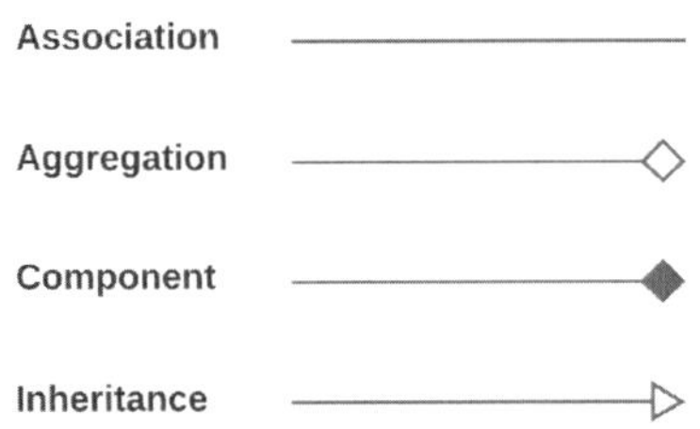

Association
Aggregation
Component
Inheritance

Figure 3.3
Types of relationships and associated line treatments

Strictly speaking, all relationships are an association (indicated by a plain line). Aggregation, component, and inheritance are specific types of associations. One approach to building a model is to connect all the objects with a plain line (showing the association) and do a second pass to identify the relationship types. However, once you get experienced with identifying relationships, you will likely find it easy to characterize them as you go along.

To learn more about relationships, we will review models that use the objects we identified in Chapter 2 (for Twitter and an e-commerce system).

Figure 3.4 shows relationships between the Twitter objects we identified previously, expanded with some additional objects to show a broader set of relationships.

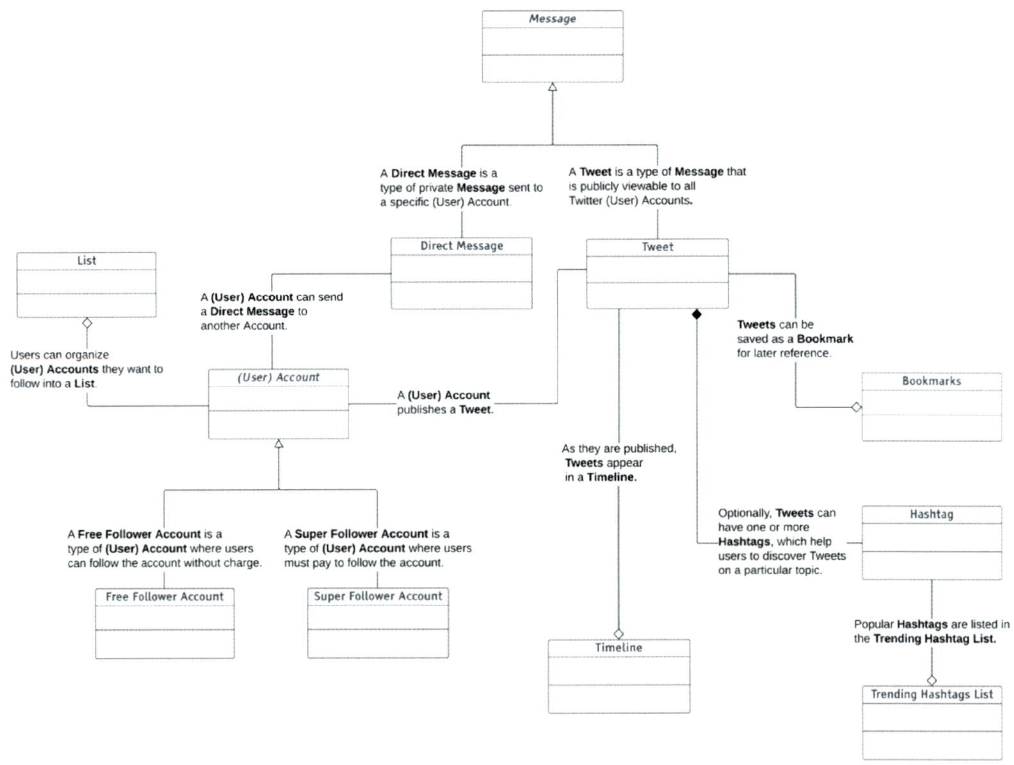

Figure 3.4

Object relationships for Twitter. You can also view this diagram at objectmodelingfordesigners.com/chapter-3

Figure 3.5 shows relationships between the e-commerce objects we've identified.

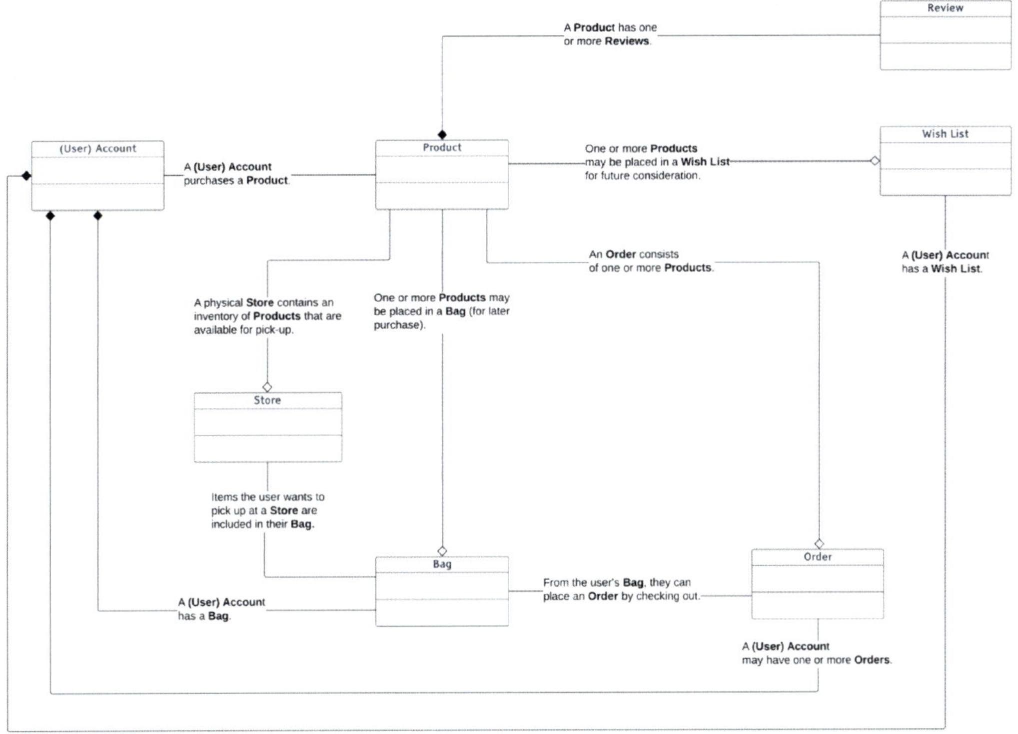

Figure 3.5
Object relationships for an e-commerce system. You can also view this diagram at objectmodelingfordesigners.com/chapter-3

Next, we'll use these example models to step through the different types of relationships.

Aggregation

An aggregation relationship indicates an object that is a group or list of other objects. The line treatment for aggregation is an open diamond, with the diamond pointing at the aggregate object.

In the Twitter model, there are four aggregate objects. Two (*Timeline* and *Bookmarks*) are associated with a *Tweet*, as shown in Figure 3.6.

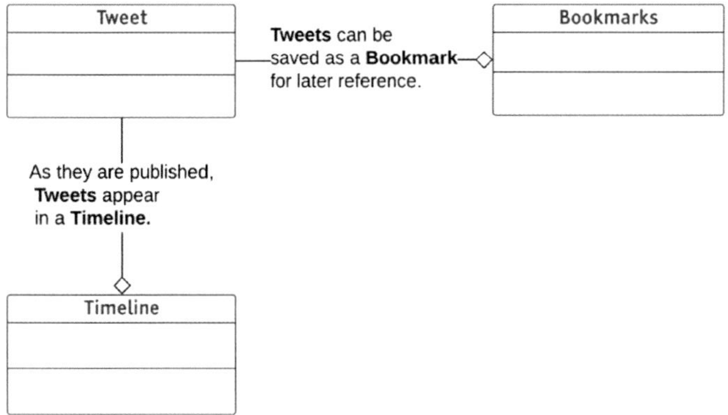

Figure 3.6
The *Timeline* and *Bookmarks* objects are aggregates of *Tweets.*

A single aggregate object (a *List*) is associated with a *(User) Account*, as shown in Figure 3.7.

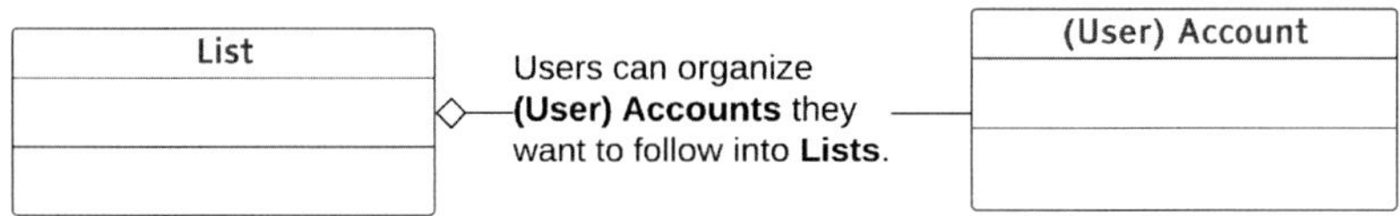

Figure 3.7
The *List* object is an aggregate of *(User) Accounts.*

Another single aggregate object (*Trending Hashtags List*) is associated with a *Hashtag*, as shown in Figure 3.8.

Figure 3.8
The *Trending Hashtags List* object is an aggregate of *Hashtags.*

In the e-commerce example, there are four aggregate objects: *Bag, Wish List, Order,* and *Store*—all of which are aggregates of *Products*, as shown in Figure 3.9.

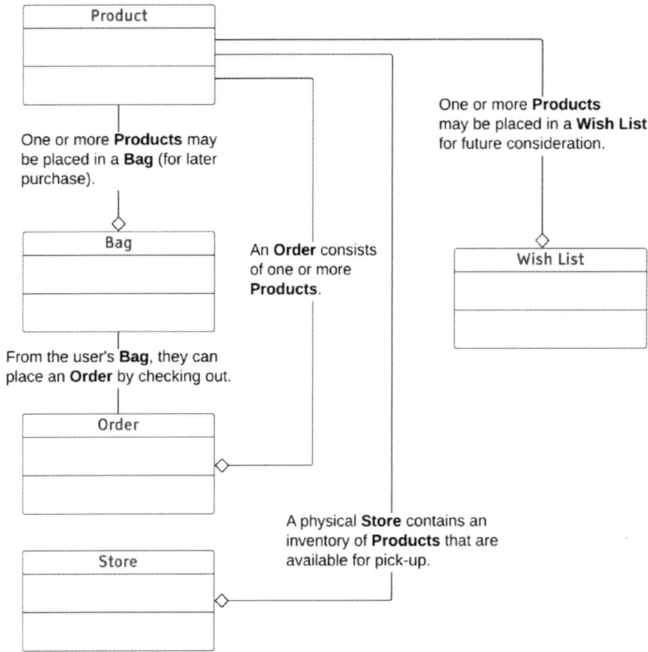

Figure 3.9
The *Bag, Order, Store,* and *Wish List* objects are all aggregates of *Products*.

Identifying aggregate objects can be extremely useful because they inherently share some basic design requirements—for example, filtering, sorting, and selecting multiple items. By looking at the design requirements of aggregate objects across the whole system, you can more easily define core conventions that will work in all contexts. Chapter 7 explains more about using relationships to define design conventions.

Component Relationship

A component relationship is a type of dependency where one object is a component of another. The line treatment for a component is a filled-in diamond attached to the object that possesses the component or components (Figure 3.10).

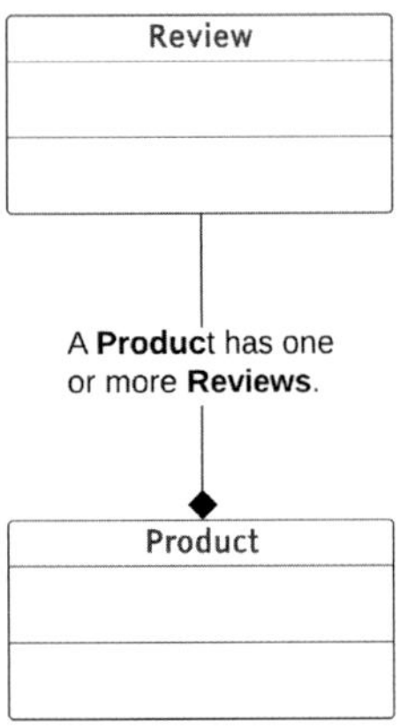

Figure 3.10
A *Review* is a component of a *Product*.

A *Review* is a component of a *Product* because the existence of a review depends on the existence of a product. If you remove the concept of product from the system, the idea of a review ceases to exist. This type of dependency indicates a component relationship.

Figure 3.11 shows an e-commerce example. There is a component relationship between User (Account) and the Bag, Wish List, and Order objects. These objects are necessarily dependent upon the existence of a User (Account).

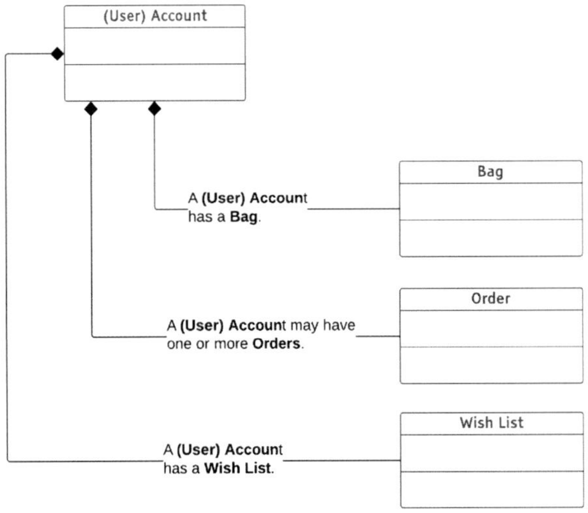

Figure 3.11
Wish List, *Order*, and *Bag* are components of a *(User) Account*.

Is It a Component—Or an Attribute?

When you model relationships, deciding whether something is a component of an object or simply an attribute of an object can be a judgment call. Attributes are covered in more detail in Chapter 5. However, as a reminder, you can consider attributes as the data fields associated with an object.

Twitter hashtags are an example of a "component versus attribute" judgment call. As shown in Figure 3.12, I chose to model *Hashtag* as a component of a *Tweet*. The reason is that the concept of a hashtag is necessarily dependent upon the concept of a tweet, meeting the criteria for a component relationship.

However, you might also consider a hashtag as an attribute of a Tweet. I chose not to model it that way for two reasons: first, hashtags are central to the Twitter experience; second, I wanted to model hashtags as aggregating into a *Trending Hashtags* List object.

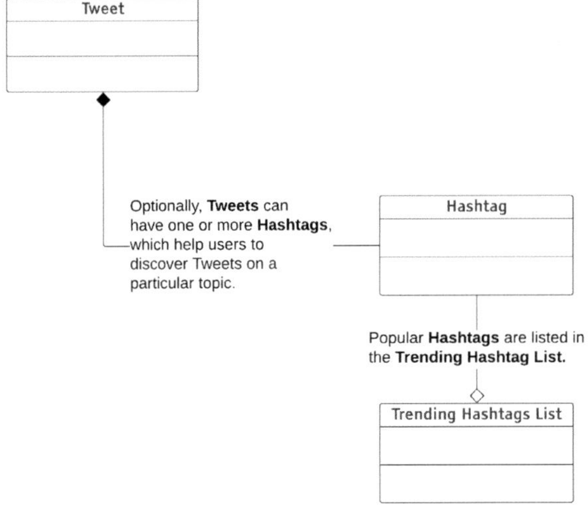

Figure 3.12
Hashtag modeled as a component of a *Tweet*

For the purpose of design, component relationships identify which objects inherently "go together" and thus appear together in the interface.

Inheritance Relationship

Inheritance indicates a parent-child relationship between two objects where the child object inherits some or all of the parent's characteristics. The line treatment for inheritance relationships is an open triangle that points at the parent object, as shown in Figure 3.13.

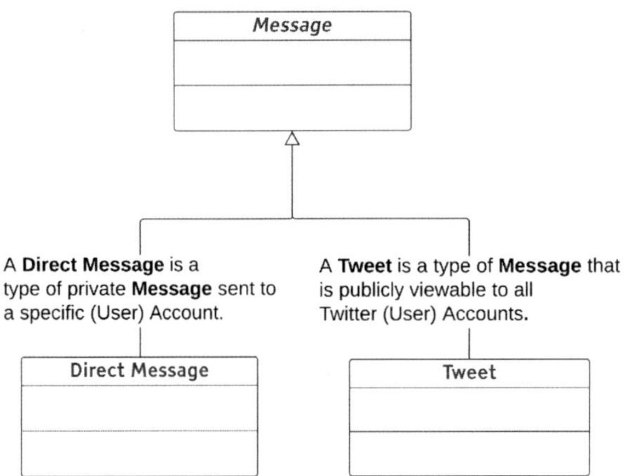

Figure 3.13
Message as the parent object of *Direct Message* and *Tweet*

On Twitter, a *Direct Message* and a *Tweet* share some specific attributes and actions, as we'll see in the following chapters. However, each object has unique characteristics as well. Shared elements are represented in the parent object; unique elements are shown in the child objects. Inheritance not only simplifies the model's presentation (you don't repeat shared elements across the child objects) but understanding inheritance relationships is also helpful when developing design conventions (covered in Chapter 7).

In Figure 3.13, *Message* is italicized because it is an abstract object, meaning there is never an instance of it. On Twitter, there are *Tweets* and *Direct Messages*; the *Message* object exists only in the model to contain the elements that the child objects share.

In Figure 3.14, we see how inheritance illustrates the different types of user accounts. *(User) Account* is an abstract object because there is never an instance of it; on Twitter, there is either a *Free Follower Account* or a *Super Follower Account.*

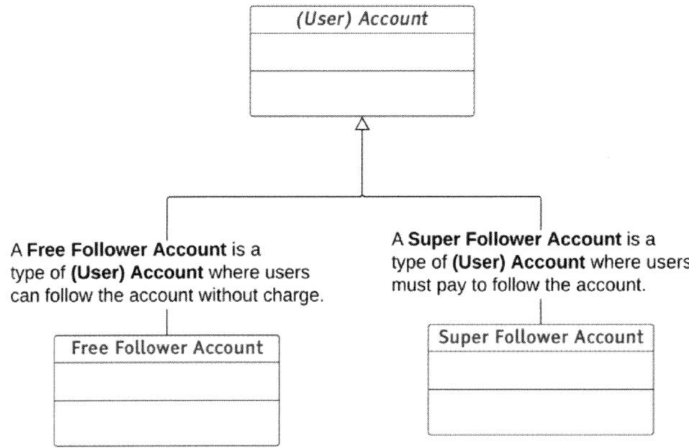

Figure 3.14
(User) Account as the parent of *Free Follower Account* and *Super Follower Account*

We've kept the example e-commerce model (Figure 3.4) simple. Still, you could imagine that *Product* could be a parent object with child objects representing different product categories (*Apparel, Housewares, Consumables*), as shown in Figure 3.15. The child objects share many characteristics (such as product name, image, price, and purchase quantity) and have some unique characteristics, such as size for *Apparel*.

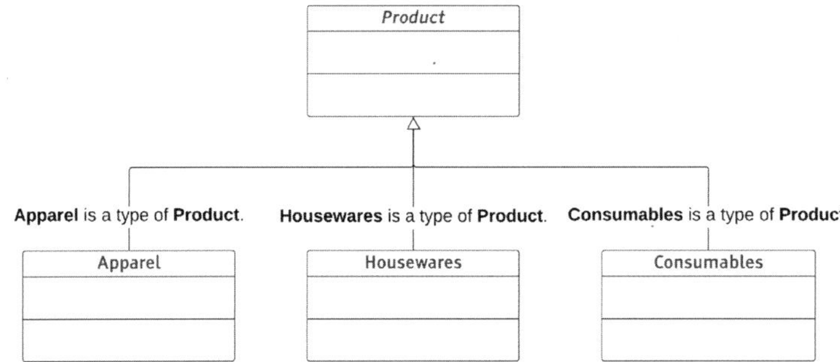

Figure 3.15
Product as the parent of *Apparel, Housewares*, and *Consumables*

Identifying Relationships

Identifying relationships between objects can be the most interesting and illuminating part of creating the model. Relationship building helps you synthesize the system's structure as a whole, which lays the groundwork for architecting the user experience.

If characterizing relationship types using the related line treatments feels too daunting, feel free to dispense with it initially or entirely. Focus on defining relationships using a simple line and describe the relationship using the narrative.

Where to Begin?

Reviewing user stories and existing interfaces can help you identify relationships. It's easiest to begin by choosing an object that is key to the experience and then build relationships out from that object. For example, the *Tweet* object is key for Twitter; the *Product* object is key for an e-commerce system.

Deciding How Many Relationships to Define

In defining relationships, you want to focus on illustrating the most important relationships. Striving for absolute completeness risks creating an impossibly complex model. Specifically, I've found that people can get tripped up by the *Account* object since it represents the user, and the user, by definition, can interact with any object in the model. As a result, I advise particular caution with the *Account* object: here, choose a few key relationships to illustrate. Keep in mind that the user's interaction with a system is fully defined in other (task perspective) artifacts such as user stories and task flows.

Identifying Relationships as a Team

As with objects, identifying relationships can be an effective team activity, using sticky notes and a large expanse of paper (such as butcher paper) or a virtual collaborative workspace. In the example below, participants identified objects using 3" x 3" sticky notes and captured relationships on larger 3" x 5" sticky notes of a different color. Then they arranged both types of sticky notes on butcher paper, drawing lines between them to indicate the relationships.

Figure 3.16
Workshop participants identifying object relationships

The advantage of identifying relationships as a team is that it encourages discussion around relationships and how they can best be characterized. For more resources on building models collaboratively, visit objectmodelingfordesigners.com/resources

Exercise B: Identifying Relationships

For this exercise, you'll use the objects identified for Slack (shown in Figure 3.17) to build relationships between the objects. Refer as needed to the Slack user stories in Exercise A or the actual Slack application. The solution to the exercise is in the next section.

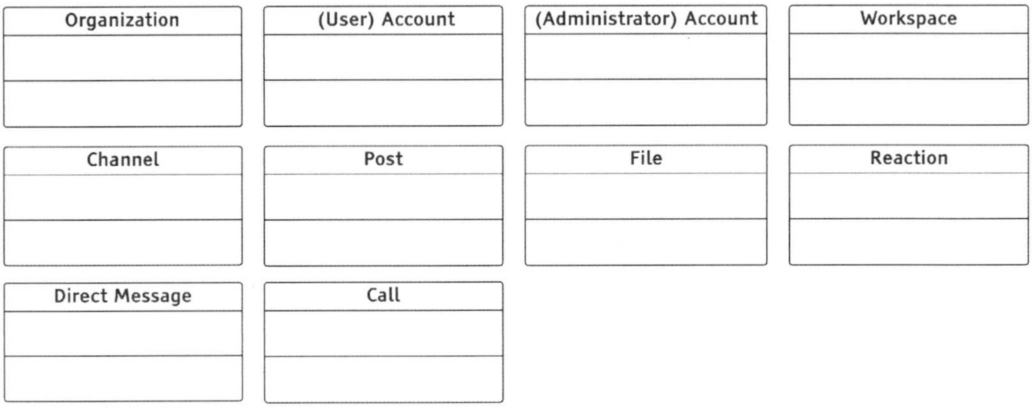

Organization	(User) Account	(Administrator) Account	Workspace

Channel	Post	File	Reaction

Direct Message	Call

Figure 3.17
Objects for Slack

Exercise B: Solution

In Exercise B, you identified relationships between the objects for Slack. Here's the example solution (Figure 3.18):

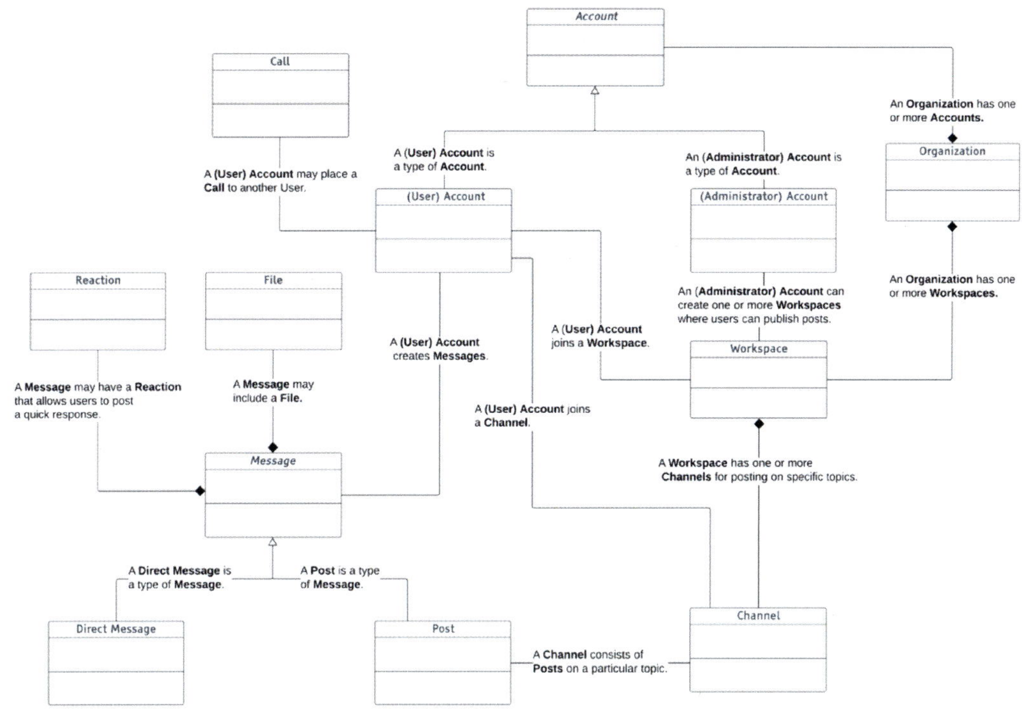

Figure 3.18
Object relationships for Slack. You can view this diagram at objectmodelingfordesigners.com/chapter-3

About the Solution

This model shows two inheritance relationships:

- (User) Account and (Administrator) Account have a parent Account object
- *Post* and *Direct Message* have a parent *Message* object

Creating these inheritance relationships anticipates that the child objects will have unique characteristics and share characteristics from their parent.

Your narrative relationship statements may differ, or you may have chosen to represent relationships that aren't shown in the sample solution. All of that is fine as no two people or teams will represent a system in precisely the same way. You do, however, want to make sure that your model conveys an accurate structural story of the system.

Note also that the model at this stage is still a work in progress. Its relationships may change as we learn more about a system or think about the object relationships differently.

Chapter 04

Actions

Thus far, we've focused on objects and their relationships, which help tell the system's structural story. We will shift to another primary model element: **actions**, which define how users interact with the objects. As mentioned earlier, while objects are the nouns of a system, actions are the verbs.

As shown in Figure 4.1, actions appear in the bottom pane of the object rectangle. For example, the *Account* object's actions are *Withdraw* and *Deposit.* As a stylistic preference, I retain the traditional notation for actions in an object model and add parentheses to the end of each action. This notation helps visually distinguish actions from the other model elements, making larger, more complex models easier to read.

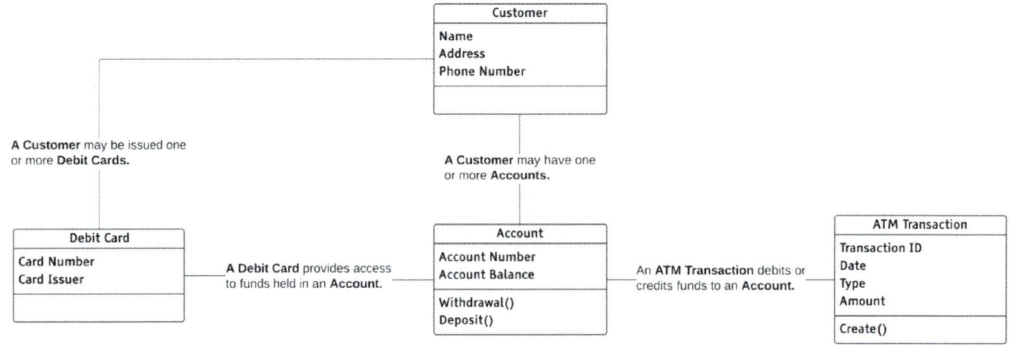

Figure 4.1
Narrative object model for an ATM. You can also view this diagram at objectmodelingfordesigners.com/chapter-4

Each set of object-action pairs represents a task in the system. And in fact, you can create a set of concise task statements from these object-action pairs:

- Withdraw from Account
- Deposit to Account
- Create an ATM Transaction

Identifying Actions

As with objects, you can identify actions by reviewing user stories or examining an existing interface.

Additionally, with actions, it's helpful to review a short checklist of standard actions for each object to check their applicability. These include a variation of the so-called CRUD actions (create, read, update, delete), plus a special *Search For* action:

- *Create*
- *Edit*
- *Delete*
- *Search For*

Create, *Edit*, and *Delete* are standard transactional actions that change an object's state. I've omitted the *Read* action from the standard CRUD list because we can assume that all objects in our model are viewable—can be "read."

I also review the applicability of the *Search For* action. It's a somewhat special case in that it acts on the entire set of object instances in the system. However, I find it helpful to indicate which objects are subject to search.

Finding Actions for the Tweet Object

Let's identify actions for the *Tweet* object, beginning with the standard transactional actions of *Create*, *Edit*, and *Delete*:

- In the case of Twitter, you can create a tweet, which is known as Tweeting; the corresponding action is *Tweet*.
- You can *Delete* a tweet (as long as it's a tweet you created).
- Famously, Twitter does not allow users to *Edit* a tweet.

Considering the Search For action, you can indeed search for tweets.
Note, however, that the actions of Tweet and Delete are available only to the tweet's author. On Twitter, the user's relationship to the tweet impacts which actions are available. In this case, we can annotate the actions, as shown in Figure 4.2.

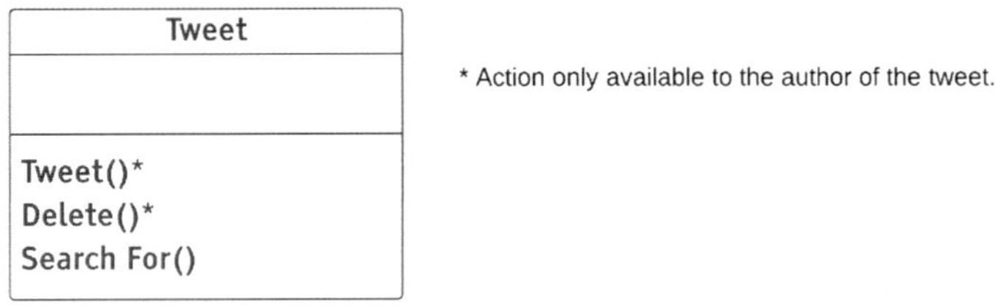

Figure 4.2
The *Tweet* object with annotated actions

In the Twitter interface, we'll first look at actions available for a tweet created by someone else (in this case, NASA). Figure 4.3 shows actions for a tweet highlighted in the top contextual menu and the bottom button bar.

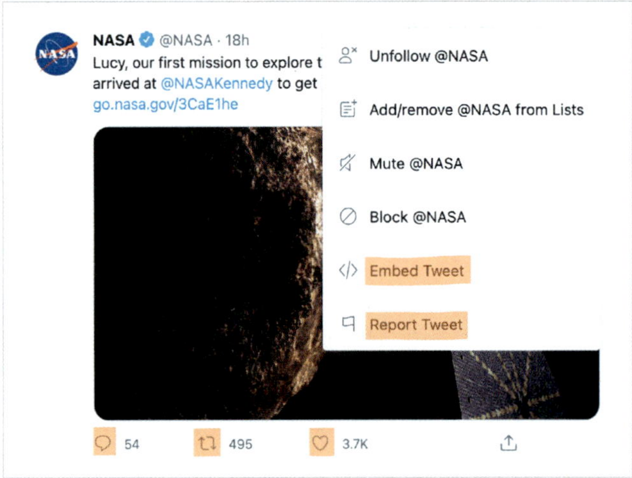

Figure 4.3
Actions identified for a tweet

Note that in the contextual menu, many of the actions act against the account object (@NASA). However, there are two actions associated with a tweet:

- *Embed*
- *Report*

For brevity and consistency in the model, we're not repeating the object's name (*Tweet*) in the action. Thus, the menu item "Embed Tweet" becomes the *Embed* action; the menu item "Report Tweet" becomes the *Report* action.

In the bottom button bar, there are three actions for a tweet:

- *Reply*
- *Retweet*
- *Like*

The last icon in the bottom toolbar displays a "more actions" menu (Figure 4.4).

Figure 4.4
The "more actions" menu

In this menu, we can identify the following actions for a tweet:

- *Send via Direct Message*
- *Add to Bookmarks*
- *Copy Link*
- *Share*

Figure 4.5 shows the actions for the *Tweet* object identified thus far:

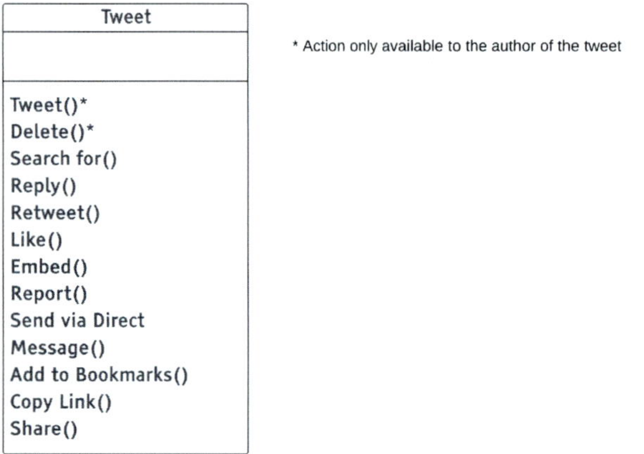

Figure 4.5

The *Tweet* object with actions

Next, we'll look at a tweet that I, as a user, created. Figure 4.6 highlights actions available for a tweet in this case:

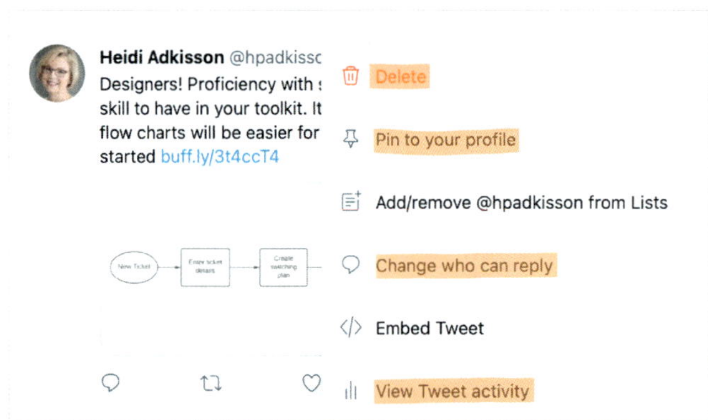

Figure 4.6

Actions available to the author of a tweet

Here, there are four additional actions:

- *Delete*
- *Pin to Your Profile*
- *View Activity*
- *Change Who Can Reply*

Figure 4.7 shows the complete set of actions identified for the *Tweet* object, with additional annotations about the role needed for specific actions (whether the user authored the tweet). I confirmed which actions were only available to the author of a tweet—and which were only available where the user is *not* the author—by checking a tweet that I authored against one created by someone I follow.

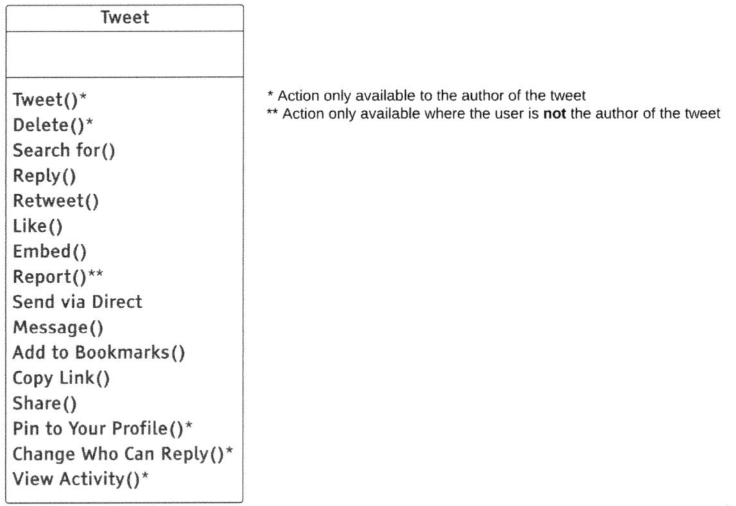

Figure 4.7
The Tweet object with actions

Identifying Actions for the Product Object

Next, using the product detail page from our example e-commerce site (Figure 4.8), we will look for actions associated with the *Product* object.

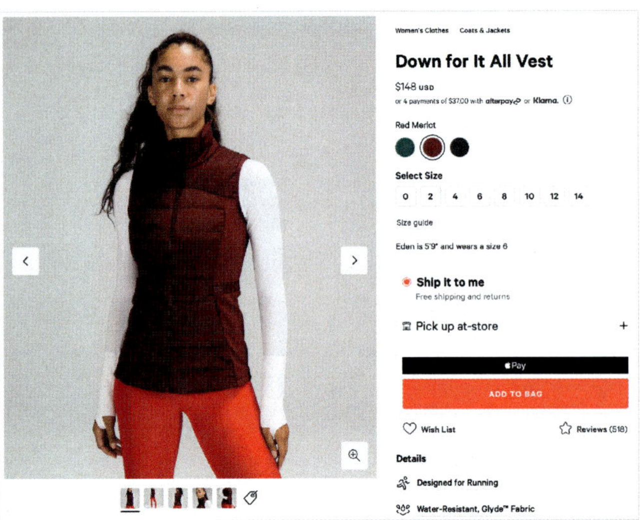

Figure 4.8
Product detail page

In reviewing the standard transactional actions (*Create*, *Edit*, *Delete*), none apply to the *Product* object in this context. There's probably a back-end system that allows the retailer to perform these functions in managing the site, but here we are representing the customer-facing experience.

In reviewing the *Search For* action's applicability, it's clearly applicable here because users should be able to search for products.

A nuance with an e-commerce site is that the experience is a mix of content navigation (for example, browsing products) and functionality (such as adding a product to a wish list or bag). An object model, in its primary intent, depicts functionality. As a result, in this case, we want to look for functional actions, not navigational links.

Looking for actions on the page (Figure 4.9), we can see that *Add to Bag* is a primary action and that a secondary action, *Apple Pay*, appears above it. There are also two tertiary actions: *Pick Up at Store* and *Add to Wish List*.

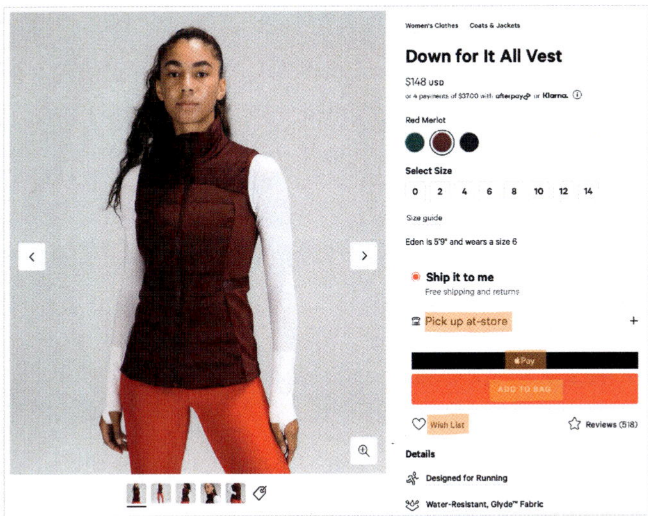

Figure 4.9
Actions for the *Product* object

When reviewing an interface for actions, remember that icons may represent all or part of an action. In the model, you want to express all actions as they would be labeled using text.

Figure 4.10 shows the actions we've identified for the *Product* object.

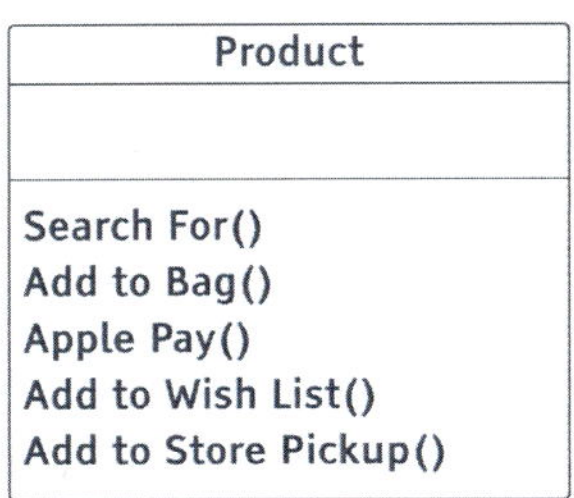

Figure 4.10
The *Product* object with actions

What about selecting a color and choosing a size? Are these actions for the *Product* object? The answer is no because color and size are attributes of a *Product*. When a user specifies color and size, they are simply changing the value of these attributes. It's helpful to consider actions as transactional (transforming the object's state) or otherwise acting directly upon the object.

Identifying Actions in User Stories

Just as we identified objects by finding nouns in the goal statement of a user story, we can discover actions by identifying the verbs. Here are the example user stories for Twitter with the actions (verbs) highlighted in light orange:

- As an unregistered user, **I want to create an account** so that I can use the service.
- As a user, **I want to send a tweet** so that I can communicate to my followers.
- As a user, **I want to add a hashtag to a tweet** so that my tweet can be grouped with other tweets that share the same hashtag.
- As a user, **I want to follow another person's account** so that I can see the tweets that they post.
- As a user, I want to see tweets from all accounts I follow in a timeline so they are all together in a single view.
- As a user, **I want to create a list of specific accounts** so that tweets from those accounts are together in a single view.
- As a user, **I want to add a tweet to my bookmarks** so I can easily refer to it later.
- As a user, **I want to send a direct message to another person's account** so that I can communicate with them privately rather than publicly.
- As a user, **I want to see a list of trending hashtags** so that I can stay up-to-date on the hottest topics.

Here are example user stories for the e-commerce website with actions similarly highlighted:

- As a user, **I want to search for products** so that I can find products that meet my needs.
- As a user, **I want to read reviews** so I can learn what other people think about the product.
- As a user, **I want to add products to my wish list** so that I can save items that I don't want to purchase now but might want to later.
- As a user, **I want to add products to my bag** so I can purchase them when I'm done shopping.
- As a user, I want to pick up products I purchase at a nearby store so that I can receive them more quickly.

- As a user, I want to submit an order for products in my bag so that I can receive them.
- As a user, **I want to create an account** so that I can have access to my order information and purchase history.
- As a user, **I want to view my orders** so I can see what I've purchased in the past.
- As a user, **I want to create a review about the product I purchased** so that I can share my opinion with potential buyers.

Example Models with Relationships and Actions

Figures 4.11 and 4.12 are the models for Twitter and the e-commerce system updated with actions. Note that these models, for illustrative purposes, aren't complete real-world systems. They are instead intended to show main representative functions. We will use the models to look in more detail at representing actions.

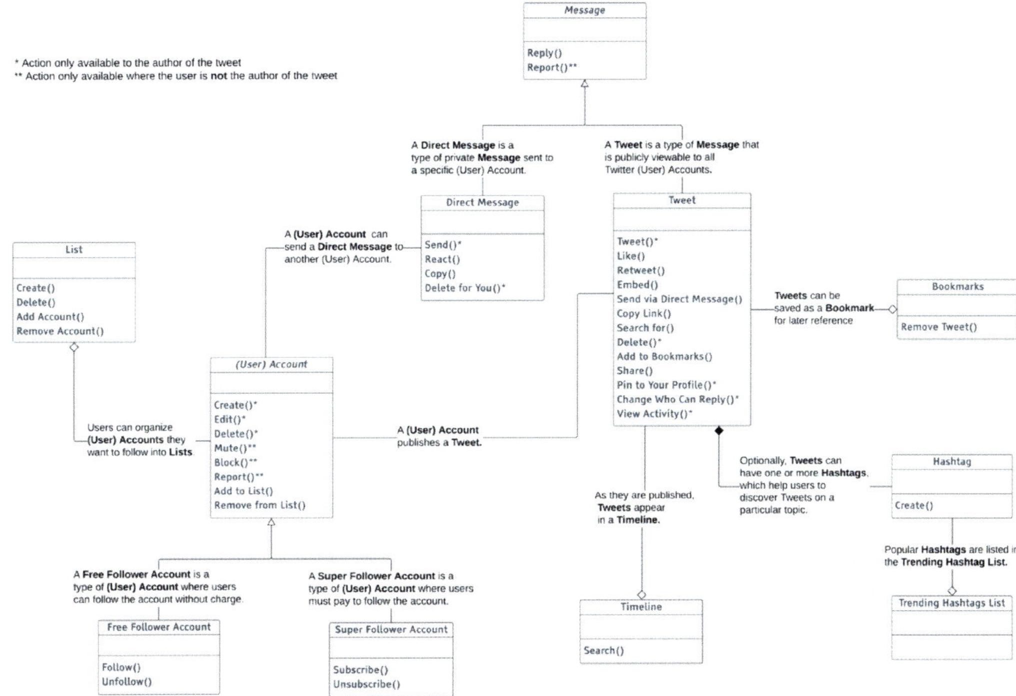

Figure 4.11

Narrative object model for Twitter including objects, actions, and relationships. You can also view this diagram at objectmodelingfordesigners.com/chapter-4

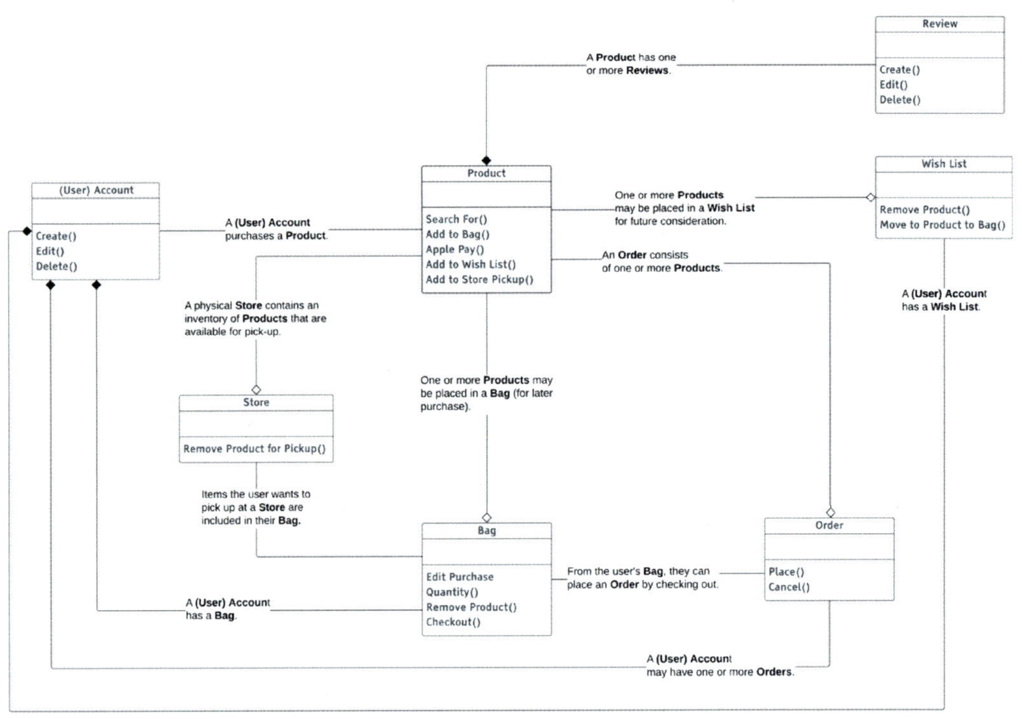

Figure 4.12
Narrative object model for an e-commerce system, including objects, actions, and relationships. You can also view this diagram at objectmodelingfordesigners.com/chapter-4

Representing Actions Where There is Inheritance

With actions now included in the models, we can see more about inheritance (Figure 4.13).

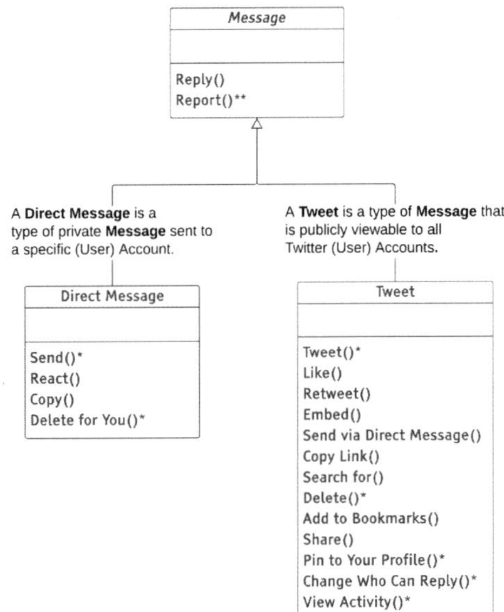

Figure 4.13
An inheritance relationship with shared actions

Figure 4.13 illustrates how the parent object contains actions shared by all the child objects; each child object contains actions that are unique to that object.

Add To and Remove Actions

The *Add To* and *Remove* actions are often present when there is an aggregation relationship between two objects:

- In general, an object can be *Added To* its corresponding aggregate.
- Conversely, it can also be *Removed* from its aggregate.

Figure 4.14 shows an example of *Add To* and *Remove* actions. A user may add a product to their wish list and later, if desired, remove it. You can see additional examples of these actions in the model with the *Bag* and *Store* objects.

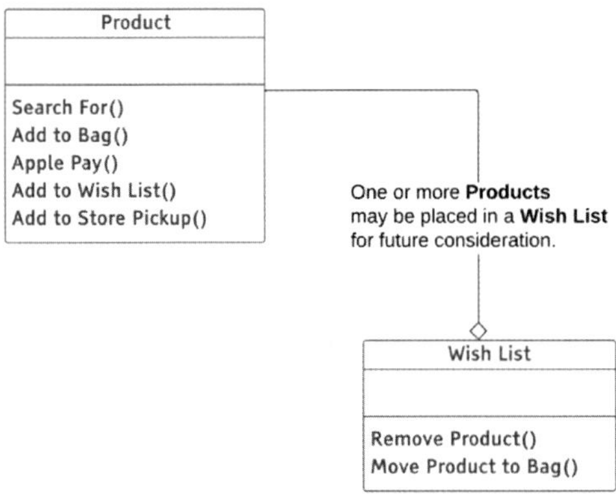

Figure 4.14
Add To and *Remove* actions associated with the *Wish List* aggregate object

A Final Tip About Modeling Actions

As mentioned earlier, it's helpful to consider actions as transactional (transforming the object's state) or otherwise acting upon the object. As such, I don't include screen-level interactions such as filter, sort, hide/show, and expand/collapse as actions in the model. These types of micro-interactions will be defined downstream in the design process. Overall, the model is most useful as a high-level representation of a system's features and functions. We will cover more specifically using the model to inform design in Chapter 7.

The Importance of Object-Action Relationships

In a well-designed interface, there is a clear relationship between an object and its associated actions. The product detail page in Figure 4.15 provides a good example: actions are clustered around the *Product* object (represented by the product image and name).

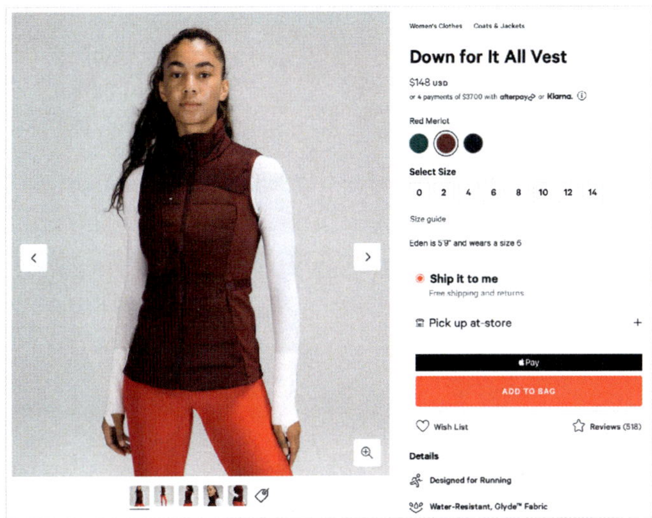

Figure 4.15
Actions associated with the *Product* object

Figure 4.16 shows how the main actions for the *Tweet* object are presented effectively in a tightly associated bottom button bar.

Figure 4.16
Actions for a Tweet on its bottom button bar

Degraded Object-Action Relationships

Most designers intuitively understand the importance of clear object-action relationships. The reality, however, is that object-action relationships can degrade, particularly in more complex or mature systems. This degradation sometimes happens when features are "tacked on" to an interface over time. Degraded object-action relationships can result in a complex architecture that is difficult for users to learn and use.

Figure 4.17 shows the original navigation for an enterprise system used to manage mortgage applications. Over time, actions associated with the key object *File* had become dispersed among seven top-level navigation options: *File Search*, *Reserve File Num*, *New File Entry*, *Quick File Entry*, *File Home Page*, *File Summary*, and *File Notes*. Overall, the system's complex navigation was a huge pain point for users and a source of employee dissatisfaction.

File Search
Reserve File Num
New File Entry
Quick File Entry
Quick Refi Entry
Customer Search
File Home Page
Sarter/Ref.
File Workflow
Terms/Dates/Status
Properties/Tax Info
File Summary
SDN Tracking Summary
Buyers
Sellers
New Loan
Payoff Loan
Assumption Loan
Real Estate Broker/Agent
Outside Escrow Company
Attorney-Buyer
Attorney-Seller
Outside Title Company
Search Vendor
Title/Escrow Fees
Escrow Charge Processes
Escrow Closing
Document Repository
Event/Tracking Log
File Notes
Generic Email

Figure 4.17
Original top-level navigation for a mortgage application system

Object modeling was central to re-architecting this system's navigational framework. Figure 4.18 is a before-and-after illustration showing how we consolidated the dispersed actions associated with the File object into a new File Summary view. With object modeling, we created a simpler, more unified user experience for this application.

Figure 4.18
Top-level navigation is simplified by consolidated dispersed actions. You can also view this figure at objectmodelingfordesigners.com/chapter-4

Keeping your object model up-to-date helps avoid degraded object-action relationships. Revisit the model when adding new functionality to ensure your model is complete and accurate. Reference the up-to-date model when incorporating new functions so you can appropriately integrate them into the architecture.

Exercise C: Identifying Actions

Below is our example set of user stories for Slack, highlighting the nouns from Exercise A. Your first task in this exercise is to go through the stories, identify the verbs, and use the identified verbs to create a set of actions for each object.

a) As an administrator, **I want to sign up for an account** so that we can use the service for our organization.
b) As an administrator, **I want to create one or more workspaces for my organization** so that we will have our own dedicated space on Slack.
c) As an administrator, **I want to invite users to join a workspace** so that they can communicate together.
d) As an administrator, **I want to create a channel** so that posts on a particular topic can be kept all together within the channel.
e) As a user, **I want to create an account** so that I can use the Slack service.
f) As a user, **I want to join a workspace** so that I can communicate with others there.
g) As a user, **I want to publish posts in a channel** so that I can communicate with others in that channel.
h) As a user, **I want to send a direct message to another user** so that we can communicate privately.
i) As a user, I want to edit a post or direct message I've already published so that I can correct any mistakes.
j) As a user, **I want to delete a post or direct message** so that people don't see posts I've changed my mind about publishing.
k) As a user, I want to attach a file to a post or direct message so that I can share it with others.
l) As a user, **I want to add a reaction to a post or direct message** so that I can quickly show a response without having to type out a message.
m) As a user, I **want to initiate a call to another user** so we can quickly talk in real-time.

Once you've identified actions from the user stories, add them to the Slack model. Also, check each object for the standard transactional actions (*Create*, *Edit*, *Delete*) and the *Search For* action.

Finally, if you have access to the Slack application, use it to find the objects we are modeling and identify any additional actions. The solution for this exercise is in the next section.

Exercise C: Solution

In Exercise C, you first used a sample set of user stories for Slack to identify actions for objects. Here is the solution:

a) As an administrator, **I want to sign up for an account** so that we can use the service for our organization.
b) As an administrator, **I want to create one or more workspaces for my organization** so that we will have our own dedicated space on Slack.
c) As an administrator, **I want to invite users to join a workspace** so that they can communicate together.
d) As an administrator, **I want to create a channel** so that posts on a particular topic can be kept all together within the channel.
e) As a user, **I want to create an account** so that I can use the Slack service.
f) As a user, **I want to join a workspace** so that I can communicate with others there.
g) As a user, **I want to publish posts in a channel** so that I can communicate with others in that channel.
h) As a user, **I want to send a direct message to another user** so that we can communicate privately.
i) As a user, I want to edit a post or direct message I've already published so that I can correct any mistakes.
j) As a user, **I want to delete a post or direct message** so that people don't see posts I've changed my mind about publishing.
k) As a user, I want to attach a file to a post or direct message so that I can share it with others.
l) As a user, **I want to add a reaction to a post or direct message** so that I can quickly show a response without having to type out a message.
m) As a user, I **want to initiate a call to another user** so we can quickly talk in real-time.

Next, you updated the Slack model with actions for each object. Figure 4.19 shows the solution.

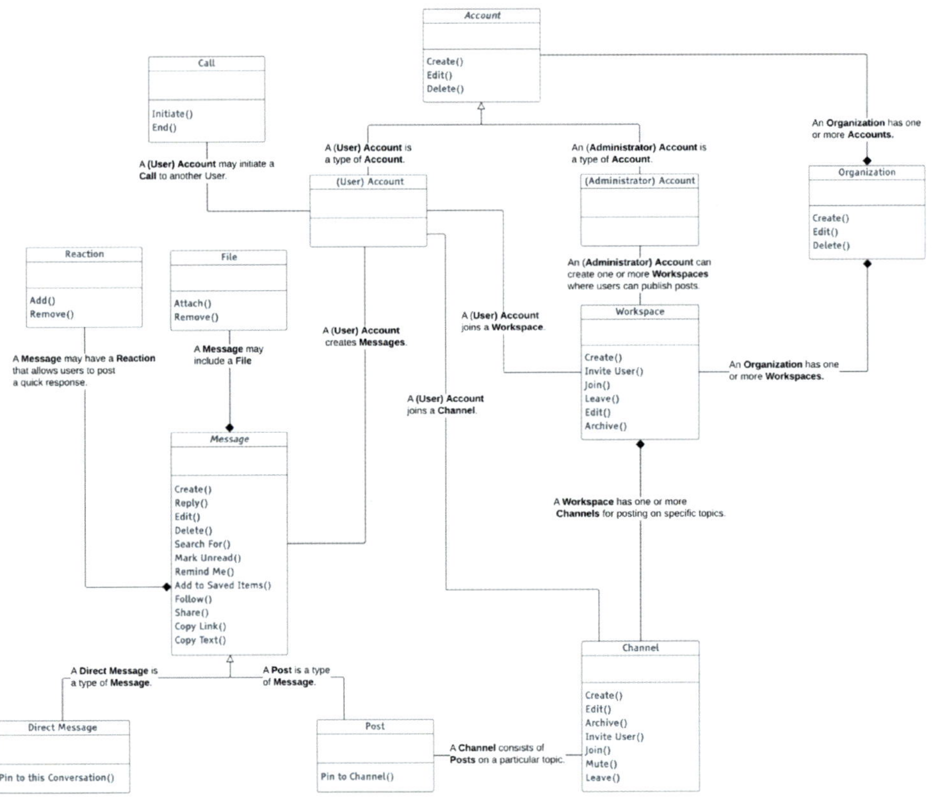

Figure 4.19

Narrative object model for Slack with objects, actions, and relationships. You can also view this diagram at objectmodelingfordesigners.com/chapter-4

About the Solution

Note that this model contains some actions that were not stated in the example user stories, including:

- Standard transactional actions (*Create*, *Edit*, *Delete*)
- The *Search For* action
- Some implied reciprocal actions (you can both *Add* and *Remove* a Reaction; *Attach* and *Remove* a File; and *Join* and *Leave* a Channel)

It also includes actions that were identified by inspecting the Slack application. Note that the (User) Account and (Administrator) Account objects have no actions listed in the lower pane. Both objects inherit their actions from the parent Account object. We'll see later that these objects do indeed have some unique attributes that warrant modeling them separately.

The above model isn't a complete representation of Slack, and its interface will likely change over time, so the specific actions in your model may differ.

Chapter 05

Attributes

There is a fourth element in the model that we've touched on but not discussed thoroughly: **attributes**. Attributes are displayed in the middle pane of each object's rectangle, as shown in Figure 5.1.

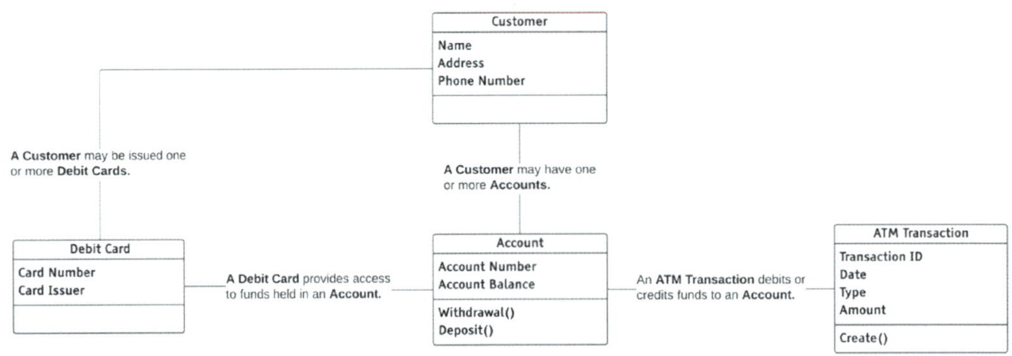

Figure 5.1
Attributes in each object's center pane. You can also view this diagram at objectmodelingfordesigners.com/chapter-5

A way to think about attributes is that they represent the fields in the database record for an object. For example, you could imagine the database record for a *Customer* containing fields for *Name*, *Address*, and *Phone Number*.

As mentioned previously, attributes define each instance of an object. In Figure 5.2, we see three instances of the *Customer* object (Jose E. Hamill, James Averett, and Tiffany Scott), each defined by its attributes.

Object

Customer
Name Address Phone Number

Instances

Jose E. Hamill 4310 Ben Street Sedalia, MO 65302 518-269-9354	Jamie Averett 2446 Taylor Street New York, NY 10013 914-598-6717	Tiffany Scott 934 Goodwin Avenue Omak, WA 98841 509-429-4885

Figure 5.2
The *Customer* object and example instances of that object

Example Models with Attributes

Figures 5.3 and 5.4 are our example Twitter and e-commerce models with attributes included. Again, these models don't represent complete real-world systems but show main representative functions. We will use these models to highlight some characteristics of attributes.

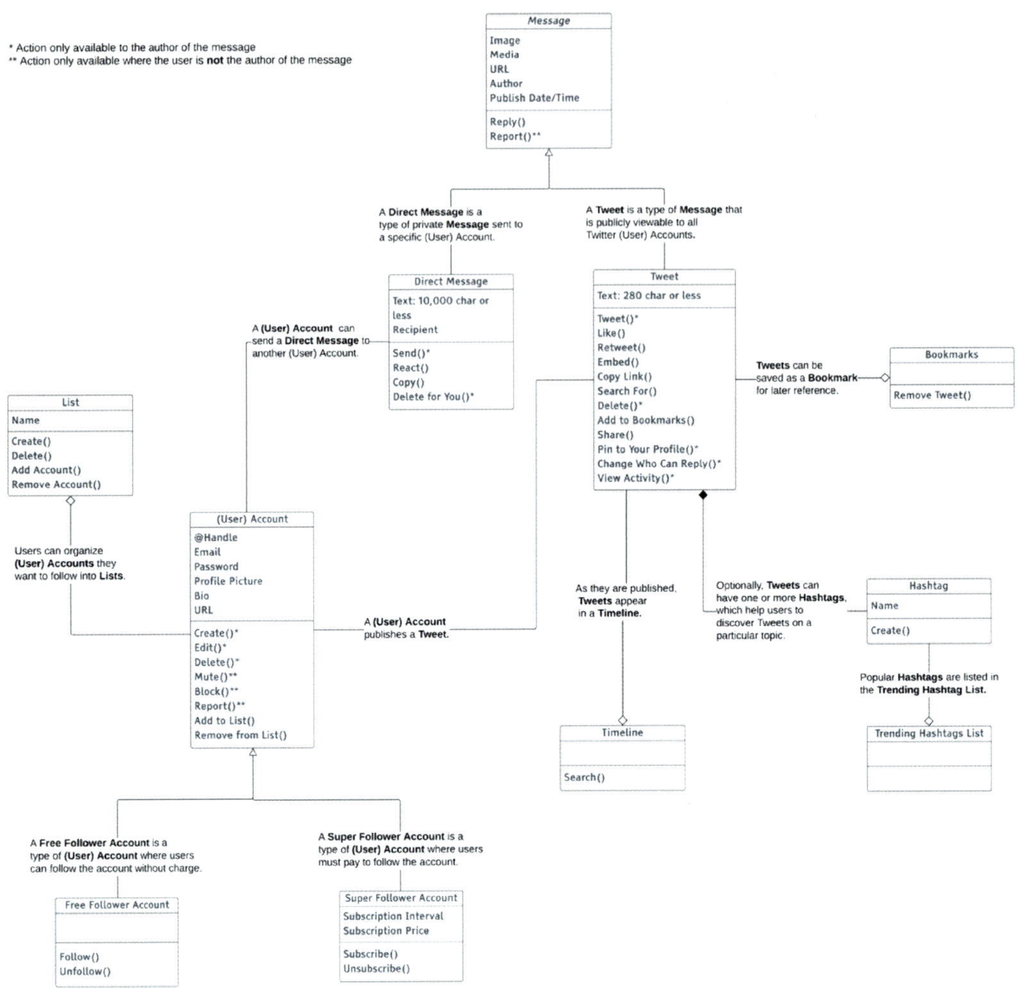

Figure 5.3

Narrative object model for Twitter, including objects, actions, attributes, and relationships. You can also view this diagram at objectmodelingfordesigners.com/chapter-5

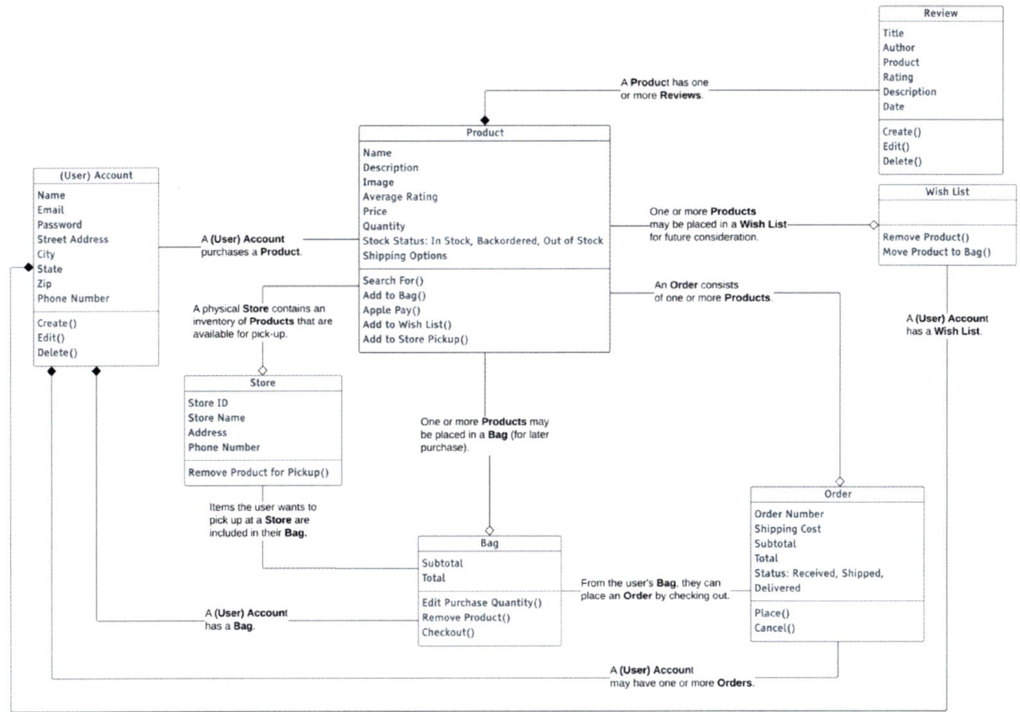

Figure 5.4

Narrative object model for an e-commerce system including objects, actions, attributes, and relationships. You can also view this diagram at objectmodelingfordesigners.com/chapter-5

Describing Attributes

Figure 5.5 shows another UML notation convention that we're adapting for our use: an **attribute description**, which appears after the attribute's name. In this example, we describe the *Text* attribute for a *Tweet* as 280 characters or less.

Figure 5.5

The *Tweet* object with the *Text* attribute

Attribute descriptions aren't usually necessary in a model, but they can sometimes make the model more useful. A tweet has a unique (and potentially unexpected) characteristic; its text is limited to 280 characters or less. In this case, it makes sense to highlight that characteristic.

Status and State Attributes

I have sometimes been asked how an object's status or state can be reflected in a model. In this case, you can use *Status* or *State* attributes.

Figure 5.6 shows a *Stock Status* attribute for the *Product* object. The value for *Stock Status* can be In Stock, Backordered, or Out of Stock. The potential values are shown as the description of the attribute.

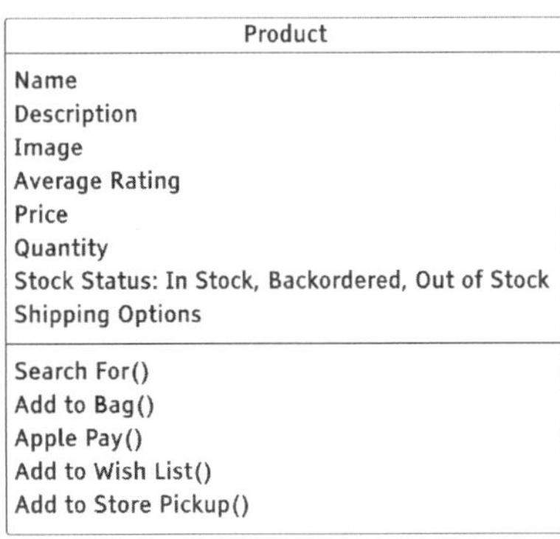

Figure 5.6
The *Product* object with a *Stock Status* attribute

Figure 5.7 is an example of a *State* attribute for a *Post* object, part of a blogging application that allows users to save a post as a draft before publishing it. In this case, there are two corresponding states: *Draft* and *Published.*

Figure 5.7
A *Post* object with a *State* attribute

In general, the values associated with *Status* and *State* attributes can be helpful to include in a model where these are important to the user experience. For example, in e-commerce, the stock status of a product is essential to users considering a purchase. Similarly, users need to quickly distinguish whether blog posts are in draft or published states.

The Role of Attributes in the Model

The advantage of including attributes in your model is that they describe more about what each object entails, which can help teams and other stakeholders understand the full role of each object in a system. Including attributes also allows you to use the model for developing or refining system vocabulary.

However, building a model with a complete set of attributes might not always make sense for your design situation. You may find that attributes are already defined elsewhere or could be more easily referenced using existing screens. Alternatively, to help better describe each object, it may suffice to include only a few key attributes rather than a complete set.

Practically, I've found that a model containing objects, actions, and relationships (minus attributes) often is enough to serve the purpose of informing design, particularly where the design work is more focused on architecting the experience.

Exercise D: Reviewing Attributes

Figure 5.8 is the model for Slack, including attributes for each object. Your task in this exercise is to review the object attributes in the model. If you have access to Slack, use the application to review how the attributes are implemented in its interface.

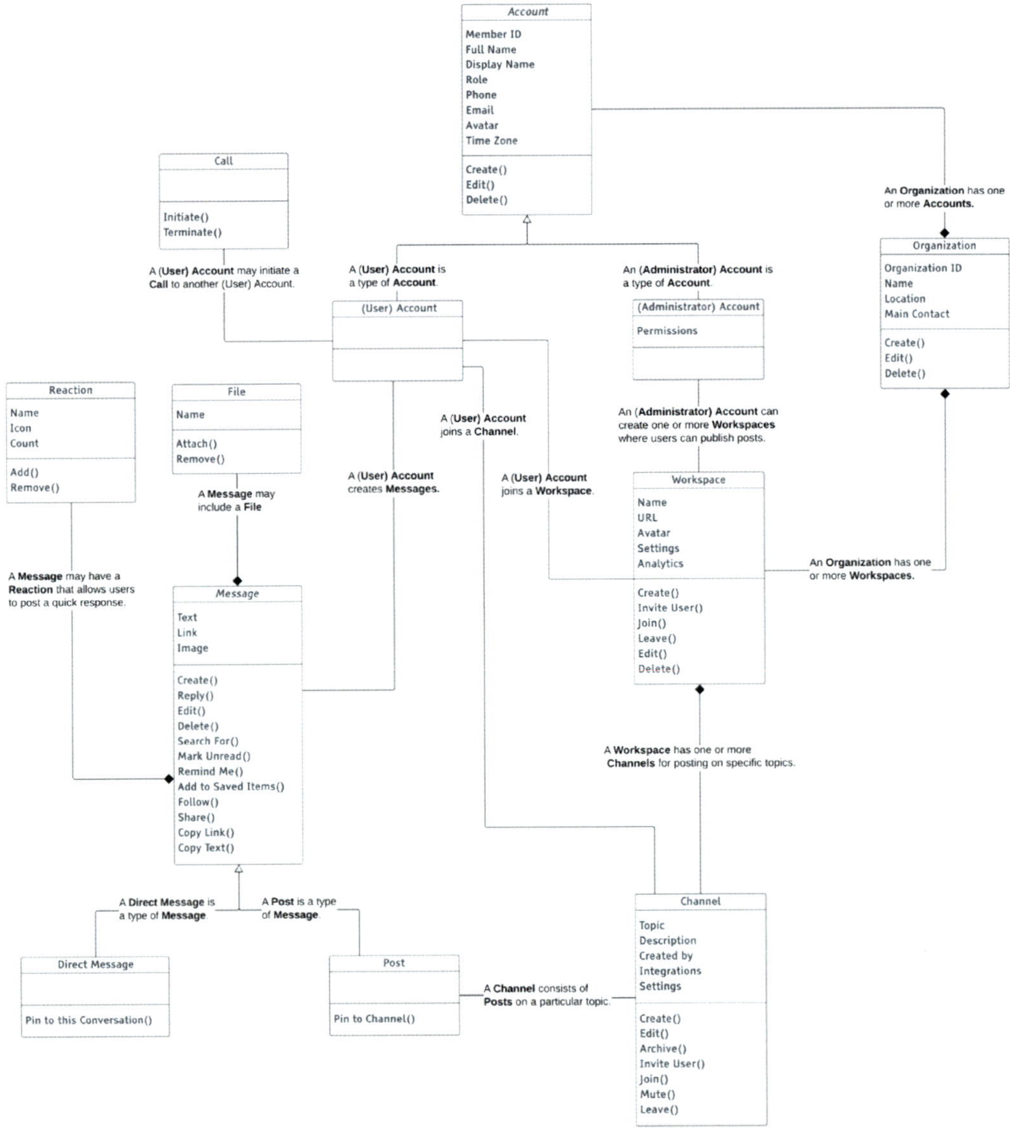

Figure 5.8

Narrative object model for Slack with objects, actions, attributes, and relationships. You can also view this diagram at objectmodelingfordesigners.com/chapter-5

"A way to think about attributes is that they represent the fields in the database record for an object."

Chapter 06

Finishing the Object Model

At this point, we've learned about objects, object relationships, actions, and attributes. Next, we will look at ways to enhance a model so it is easier to understand, particularly for those who weren't involved in creating the model. Enhancements can include visual cues that identify objects with a similar purpose or are otherwise central to the user experience. You may also want to indicate planned functionality and add explanatory annotations about the model.

Figures 6.1 and 6.2 are enhanced versions of our example Twitter and e-commerce models.

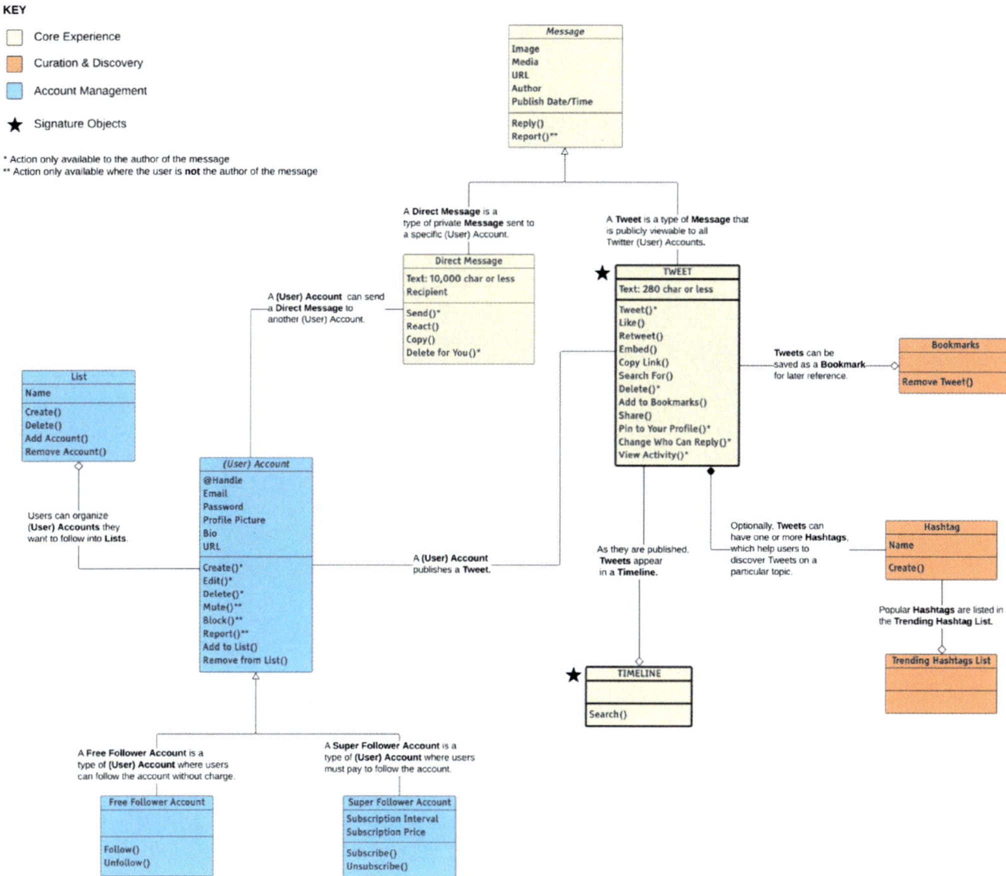

Figure 6.1

Enhanced narrative object model for Twitter. You can also view this diagram at objectmodelingfordesigners.com/chapter-6

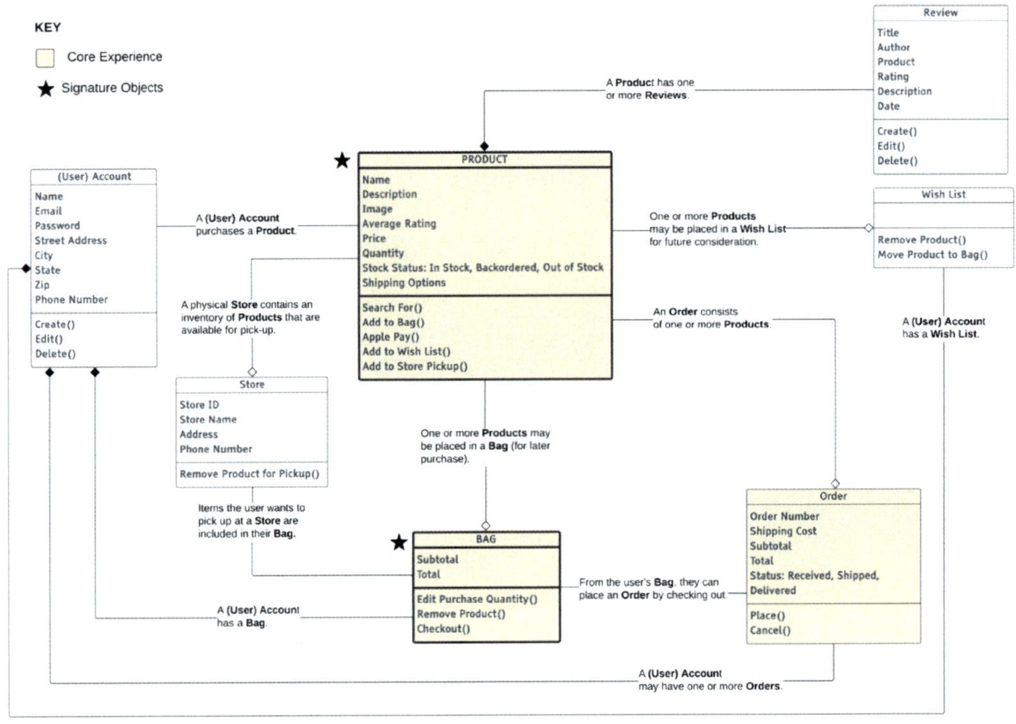

Figure 6.2

Enhanced narrative object model for an e-commerce system. You can also view this diagram at objectmodelingfordesigners.com/chapter-6

Highlighting Objects That Share a Similar Function or Purpose

Particularly for more complex models, it's helpful to use color or some other visual cue to call out objects with a similar function or purpose. In Figure 6.1 (above), there are three categories of objects:

- Core Experience (yellow)
- Curation & Discovery (orange)
- Account Management (blue)

In Figure 6.2 (also above), objects associated with the core purchase experience are highlighted in yellow.

Making a visual association between objects makes the model easier to read and useful when developing design conventions (discussed in the next chapter).

Identifying Signature Objects

Not every object is of equal importance in a system. Some objects represent a system's unique value proposition or are otherwise central to the experience; I consider these to be **signature objects.** In our enhanced models, signature objects are indicated by a star icon. For Twitter (Figure 6.1), *Tweet and Timeline* are signature objects; *Product* and *Bag* are signature for e-commerce (Figure 6.2).

Identifying signature objects helps bring forward the most important aspects of a system's user experience. Our example models are relatively simple, and their signature objects may seem obvious. However, in more complex systems, discussion around which objects are "signature" can help teams align, at a high level, on priorities for the experience.

Indicating Future Functionality

You may also want to indicate future functionality in the model. Figure 6.3 shows the case where Twitter will implement the super follower account in a future release. The *Super Follower Account* object is light gray and has a dotted outline to represent it is a feature that Twitter will develop later in the product's roadmap.

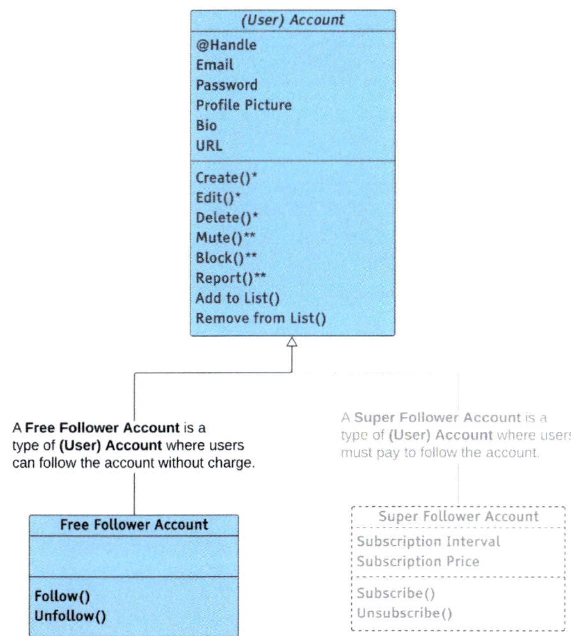

Figure 6.3
Super Follower Account designated as future functionality

Annotations

Consider what type of annotations would be helpful to clarify the model or the thought process that went into it. For example, in the Twitter model (Figure 6.1), we've added an annotation about permissions for specific actions. Particularly if you've developed the model as a team, it can be helpful to note modeling decisions that might not be clear to others. For example, for Twitter, I chose to model a *Hashtag* as a separate object rather than an attribute of a *Tweet*—this decision is something that I could have annotated as part of the model.

Also, keep in mind that there is a lot of flexibility in the relationships statements to provide more context about objects, their purpose, and intended functionality. Figure 6.4 is an example of this kind of expanded relationship statement.

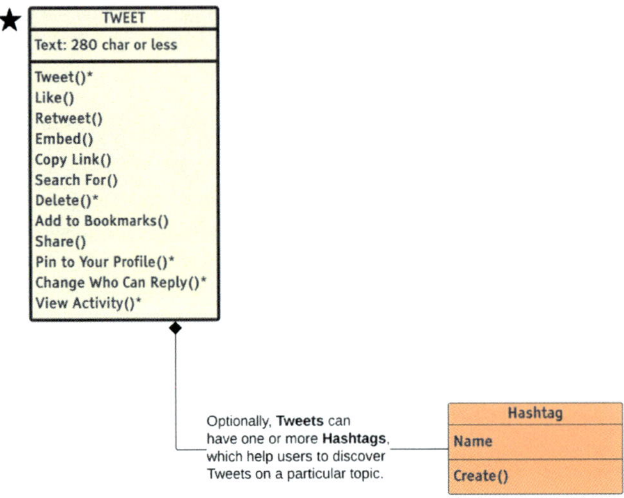

Figure 6.4
Example of an expanded relationship statement

Get Creative!

Above are just some ideas on enhancing your model to communicate more clearly. Feel free to get creative: add whatever elements or visual treatments best serve your purpose.

Exercise E: Enhancing a Model

Review the final example Slack model (Figure 6.5) and think about how you would enhance it to make it easier to use and understand. A solution is in the next section.

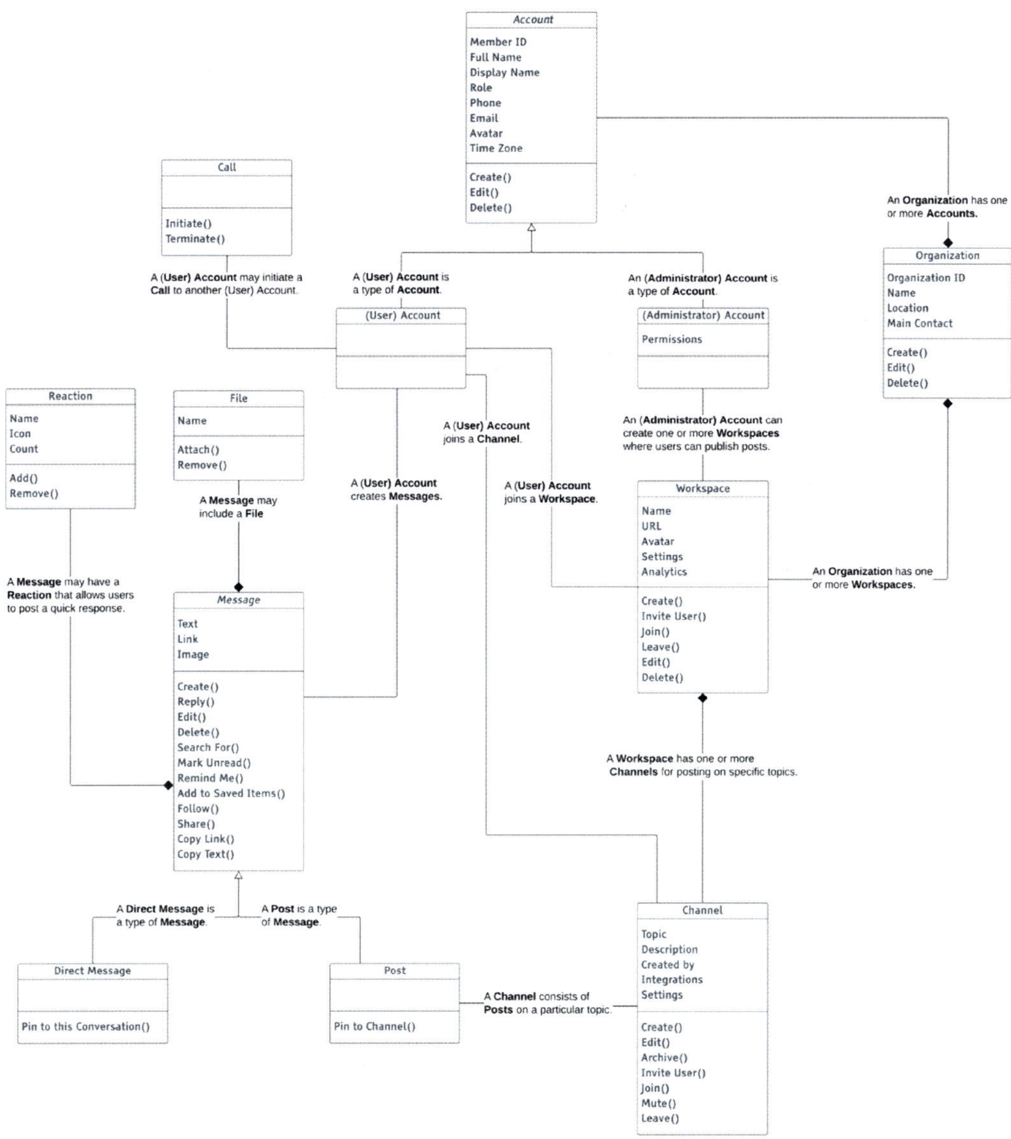

Figure 6.5

Narrative object model for Slack with objects, actions, attributes, and relationships. You can also view this diagram at objectmodelingfordesigners.com/chapter-6

Exercise E: Solution

In Exercise E, you considered how you would enhance the Slack model. Figure 6.6 shows an example solution.

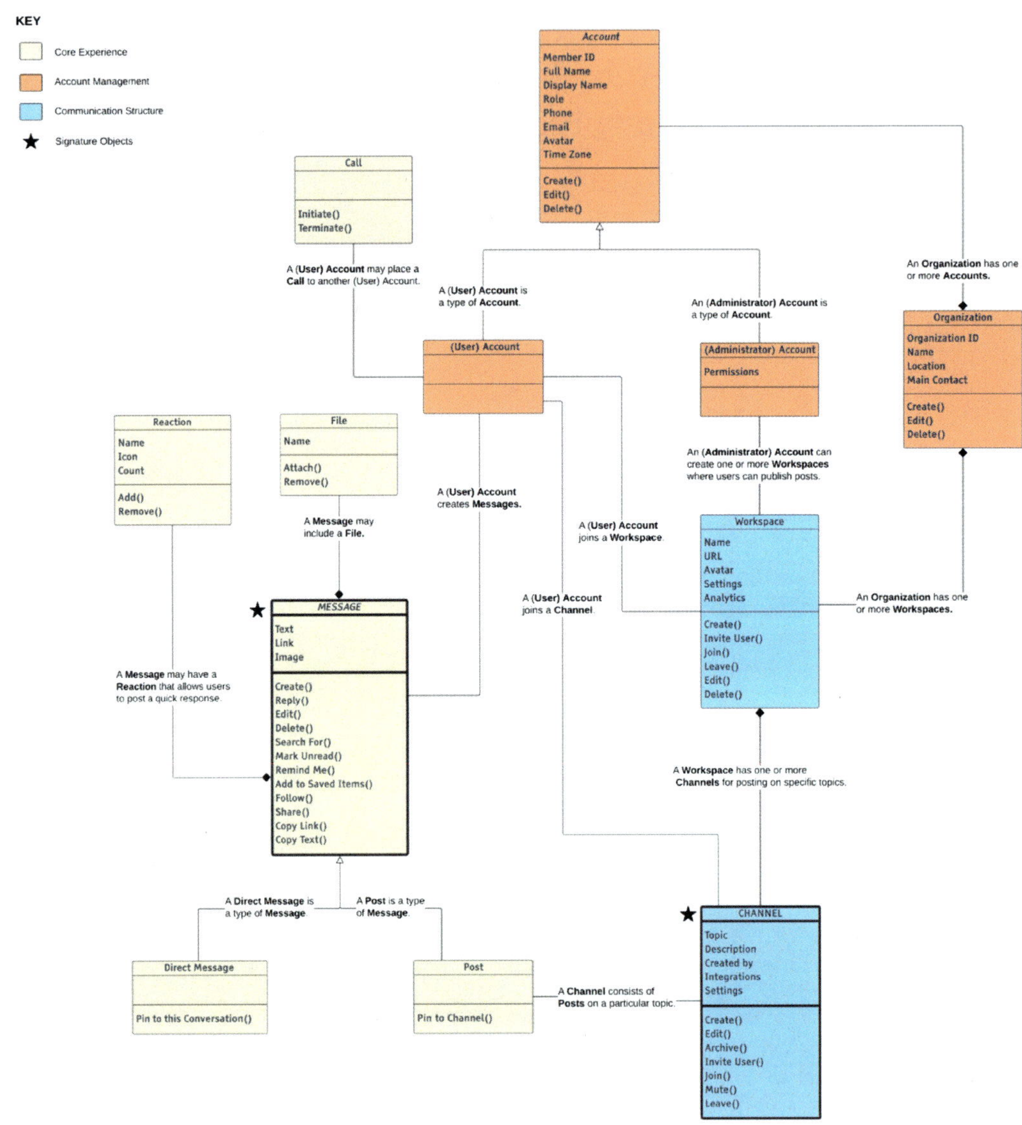

Figure 6.6

Enhanced narrative object model for Slack. You can also view this diagram at objectmodelingfordesigners.com/chapter-6

About the Solution

For Slack, I began by considering how I might group objects according to function. I could see that there were objects devoted to actively communicating with others (shown in yellow), objects that helped organize messages (shown in blue), and objects for managing accounts (shown in orange).

In addition, I wanted to highlight the signature objects *Message* and *Channel* as being central to the Slack experience.

Tips for Real-World Modeling

Through my consulting work, I've had the opportunity to create object models in all kinds of project situations. I've also had the chance to teach object modeling to others. Along the way, I've gathered some tips for real-world modeling.

Learn by Doing

Object modeling takes practice: the best way to learn is by doing. If you are in the midst of a project, consider going back and creating an object model, even if you're well along in the design process. If you don't have a current project and want some practice, find a system to model—similar to what we did here for Twitter, e-commerce, and Slack.

Define What You Want to Achieve with the Model

Think about what you want to achieve with the model. Building a full model complete with all objects, attributes, actions, and relationships is not always necessary.

For example, you might want to create a model focused solely on objects and their relationships if you are trying to capture the scope of a poorly documented legacy system.

Suppose there is a problem with dispersed actions, similar to the example shown in Figure 4.17, you might focus strictly on inventorying objects and their associated actions. In this case, rather than defining relationships, you can roughly arrange objects as you would in an affinity diagram (putting related objects closer to one another).

Another situation where you might forgo defining relationships is where your goal is to normalize system vocabulary; here, you might focus on comprehensively documenting objects, actions, and attributes.

Be Flexible in How You Build the Model

Necessarily, the first step in creating an object model is identifying the objects. You can build the other elements of the model (relationships, actions, attributes) in any order. Feel free to build the model in the way that makes the most sense to you or the given circumstances.

Build Over a Series of Shorter Work Sessions

Building a model in one long marathon work session is usually ineffective (and impractical). The advantage of working across several shorter work sessions is that it gives you time to step away from the model and look at it again with fresh eyes. Sometimes a part of the model you might have struggled with representing will become apparent on a second look.

Collaborate!

Building an object model can be an effective team exercise to get a shared understanding of either an existing system or the requirements for new functionality. For resources around team modeling, visit objectmodelingfordesigners.com/resources

Accept There is No Single "Right" Model

It's important to understand that two people may model a system slightly differently, particularly in characterizing object relationships, and that's OK. There is no one correct answer to how a system should be modeled. I have sometimes been surprised and delighted in workshops when teams model a system in a way that makes sense but differs from how I had done it.

Go for Good Enough

Remember that the goal is not to create the perfect model; avoid the trap of analysis paralysis. It's OK not to have every corner of the model 100% worked out. Instead, focus on creating a model that serves your purpose—and not more.

Have Fun!

I advise going into the modeling process with a sense of fun and adventure, to enjoy the discovery and clarity that object modeling can provide, particularly in a team situation.

Object Modeling Quick Reference

The quick reference guide may also be viewed or downloaded at objectmodelingfordesigners.com/resources

Object Modeling Quick Reference

Product
Name Description Image Average Rating Price Quantity Stock Status: In Stock, Backordered, Out of Stock Shipping Options
Search For() Add to Bag() Apple Pay() Add to Wish List() Add to Store Pickup()

Objects are the nouns in a system.

Attributes charactertize instances of an object.

Actions are the verbs.

Relationships tell the structural story of the system, illustrating which objects are closely related and which have little or no relationship with one another.

Strictly speaking, all relationships are an association (indicated by a plain line). Aggregation, component, and inheritance are specific types of associations.

Association

Aggregation

Component

Inheritance

An **aggregation relationship** indicates an object that is a group or list of other objects. The line treatment for aggregation is an open diamond, with the diamond pointing at the aggregate object.

A **component relationship** is a type of dependency where one object is a component of another. The line treatment for a component is a filled-in diamond attached to the object that possesses the component or components.

Inheritance indicates a parent-child relationship between two objects where the child object inherits some or all of the parent's characteristics. The line treatment for inheritance relationships is an open triangle that points at the parent object.

Tips

Define What You Want To Achieve With the Model
Think about what you want to achieve with the model. Building a full model complete with all objects, attributes, actions, and relationships is not always necessary.

Go for Good Enough
Remember that the goal is not to create the perfect model; avoid the trap of analysis paralysis. It's OK not to have every corner of the model 100% worked out. Instead, focus on creating a model that serves your purpose—and not more.

Be Flexible in How You Build the Model
The first step in creating an object model is necessarily identifying the objects. You can build the other elements of the model (relationships, actions, attributes) in any order. Feel free to build the model in the way that makes the most sense to you or the given circumstances.

Have Fun!
Go into the modeling process with a sense of fun and adventure—to enjoy the discovery and clarity that object modeling can provide.

"Enhancing a model makes it easier to understand, particularly for those who weren't involved in creating the model."

Chapter 07

Using the Object Model

An object model provides a concise, compact view of a system. If you created the model as a team, you have the benefit of having a shared understanding of the system. The model can also help onboard new team members, particularly if it has clear relationship descriptions.

But the primary intent of the model is to inform design and to create a system that ultimately works well for its users, is easy to develop, and is extensible into the future. This chapter will look at how to use the model to solve different design challenges, including using the model to drive design conventions.

Identifying Signature Elements

The rise of ready-made design systems such as Google Material Design means it's easier than ever for an organization to get started on a design system. However, using publicly available components (or deriving from them) can result in a system that lacks a distinctive look and feel.

A way to avoid this fate is by identifying signature elements—elements central to the experience—and making the design of those elements distinctive. The signature elements drive conventions for secondary and tertiary elements. This approach has been proposed both by Dan Mall in his article "Distinct Design Systems" and by Emmet Connolly in his blog post "The Full-Stack Design System."

The last chapter identified signature objects for Twitter (*Tweet* and *Timeline*) and the e-commerce system (*Product* and *Bag*). If we were designing Twitter from scratch or considering a major redesign, we would start by creating a distinctive design for the signature objects of *Tweet* and *Timeline.* Distinct elements might include color, iconography, motion, or interaction patterns. We could then extend the distinctive elements to similar but more secondary objects, such as *Direct Message* and *Bookmarks.* Similarly, for the e-commerce system, distinctive design elements developed for the signature objects *Product* and *Bag* could be extended to more secondary objects such as *Review* and *Wish List.*

The overall goal is to create an experience that feels distinctive, reflects the system's brand, and is more memorable than one built from publicly available components.

Building a Design System

Design systems usually start as a set of lower-level components, such as buttons and data entry controls, that ultimately roll up into higher-level design constructs (such as page archetypes or different types of data views). However, sometimes design systems get "stuck" at the component level, and never evolve to include the more complex system elements critical to creating a consistent experience.

Understandably, lower-level components are easier to implement, especially when using off-the-shelf libraries. Creating a set of higher-level design system constructs requires thought and effort, particularly deciding what elements make sense to include. In this, an object model can help. In the following sections, we will use aggregation and inheritance relationships to identify objects that likely share design requirements; these shared requirements can be represented as a design system element.

Using Aggregate Objects

Aggregate objects (as highlighted in Figure 7.1) are a top candidate for objects that potentially share similar design requirements.

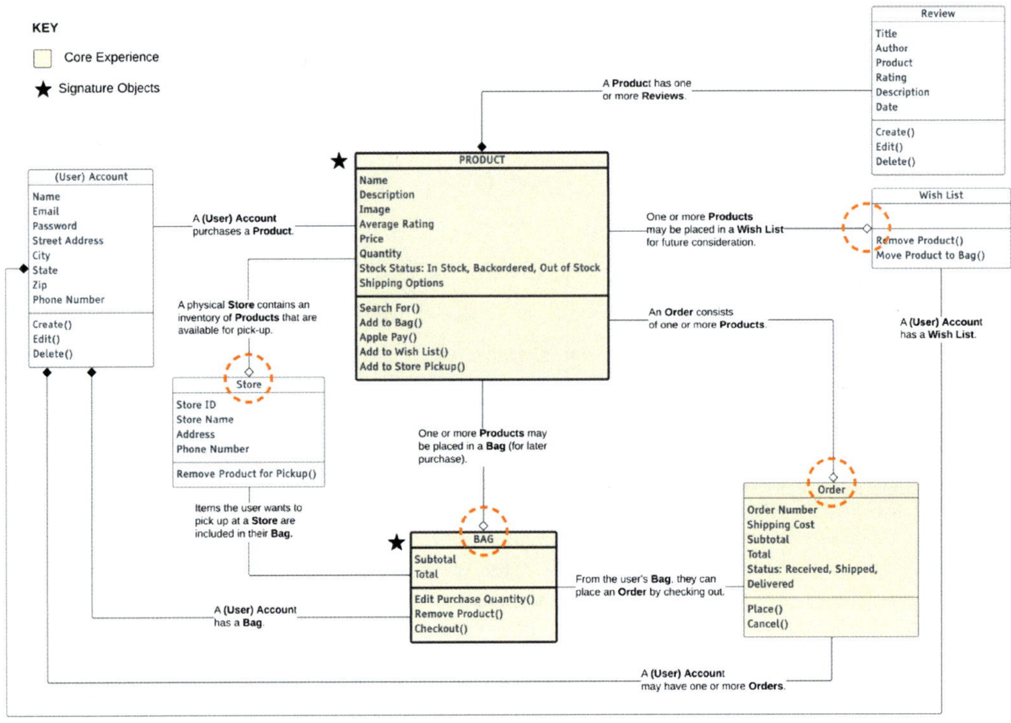

Figure 7.1

Aggregate objects in the e-commerce model. You can also view this diagram at objectmodelingfordesigners.com/chapter-7

By definition, aggregate objects are collections of other objects typically represented in an interface in some combination of a list, table, or grid view. They often share requirements for:

- Switching between the type of view (list, table, or grid)
- Filtering and sorting
- Item selection
- Taking action on one or more items

The object model allows you to see all the aggregate objects quickly, evaluate design needs across all those objects, and then abstract those needs into design system constructs.

Using Parent Objects

In an inheritance relationship, there are two or more child objects that share characteristics of the same parent. As shown in Figure 7.2, there is a parent *Message* object in Twitter; its two child objects are *Direct Message* and *Tweet*. Therefore, a design system could contain a *Message* construct that is extensible to the child objects.

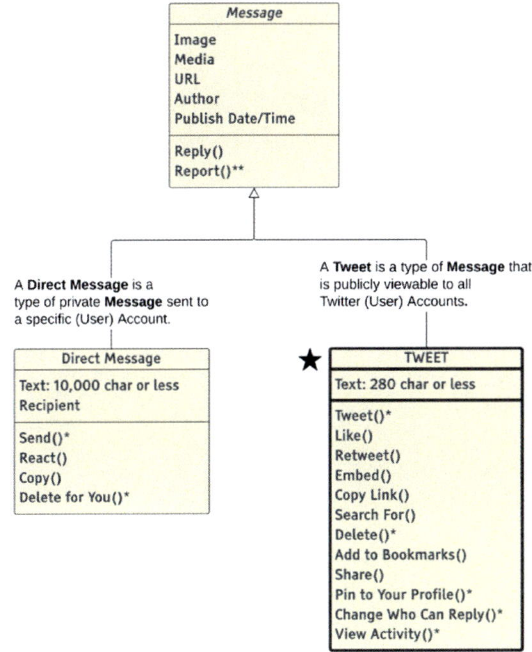

Figure 7.2
The parent *Message* object and its two children, *Direct Message* and *Tweet*

Let's consider a different example. A system used for managing mortgage applications originally used differing screen layouts for each role involved in the transaction (for example, buyer, seller, agent) even though as "people" they shared many characteristics. When creating the object model, we were able to identify a *People* parent object whose children included *Buyer*, *Seller*, *Buyer's Agent*, *Seller's Agent*, *Loan Officer*, and *Loan Assistan*t. Defining a *People* component in the design system helped us create a much more unified experience.

System Vocabulary

Clear and consistent system vocabulary is sometimes an overlooked (yet easily fixed) factor in system usability. Even seemingly equivalent terms (such as edit and update) can cause users to second-guess. Over time, inconsistent labels can creep into a system, particularly in larger, more complex systems. If you have an existing system that has grown organically over time, it can be worth modeling it to capture its current state and inventory the terms in use. You can also model a yet-to-be-developed system to help establish the system vocabulary.

Checking Vocabulary Across Objects

Start by using the model to look at similar or identical concepts that use different labels. You may find differences that require correction, or you may find some differences that are warranted. For example, Figure 7.3 shows that the "create" concept is labeled differently for a *Tweet* than a *Direct Message*. In the case of a *Tweet*, the action is *Tweet*, and for a *Direct Message*, the action is *Send*. Even though these actions would seem functionally equivalent, the labeling difference, in this case, is justified. When you create a tweet, you publish it to the world, known as tweeting (a big part of Twitter's brand identity). Creating a direct message is different, more similar to other person-to-person messaging functions.

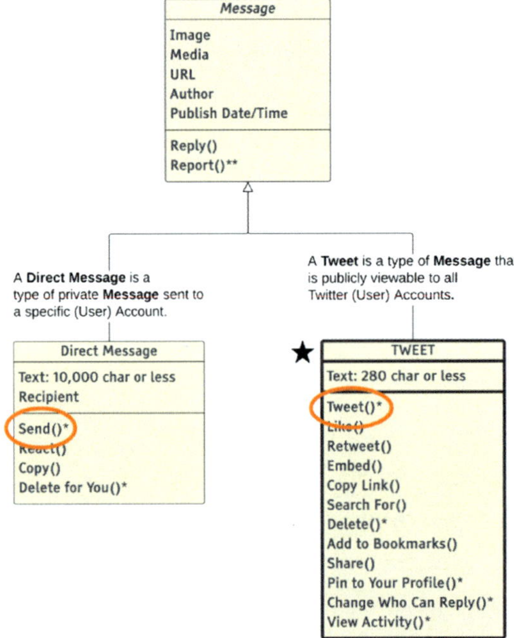

Figure 7.3
The "create" actions for a *Direct Message* and a *Tweet*

Checking Vocabulary Within Objects

It's also helpful to check the terms within an object to ensure that they all make sense. Figure 7.4 shows that the *Tweet* object uses "tweet" as a noun and a verb. We established above that the action *Tweet* makes sense, so the overlap here isn't a problem. This example is a unique circumstance, but it illustrates the type of conflicts you can identify by examining terms within an object. Overall, it can be helpful to double-check each object and the terms it uses for its actions and attributes.

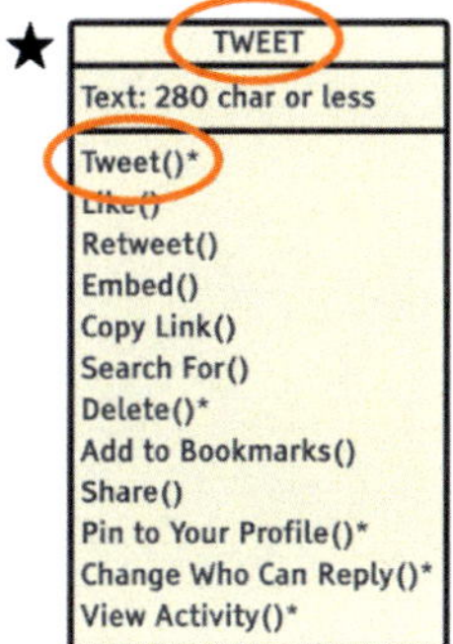

Figure 7.4
Tweet as both an object and an action

Checking for Functional Completeness

The object model can provide a helpful cross-check that all objects are functionally complete, and that actions, in particular, haven't been overlooked.

Recall the short list of standard actions we reviewed when creating a model:

- *Create*
- *Edit*
- *Delete*
- *Search For*

These actions are a great starting point to check for functional completeness.

We did find a potential case of an object being functionally incomplete with the *Tweet* object. Famously, Twitter doesn't allow users to edit a tweet once they post it. In this case, the lack of edit functionality is intentional, but it could also have been overlooked.

Additionally, it can be helpful to look at objects that serve a similar purpose and compare them. Do similar objects have similar functions? Should they?

For example, in Twitter, the *Tweet* and *Direct Message* objects serve a similar purpose—to communicate with others. As shown in Figure 7.5, you can *Like* a tweet, but you can't *Like* a direct message. Should users be able to *Like* a direct message as well?

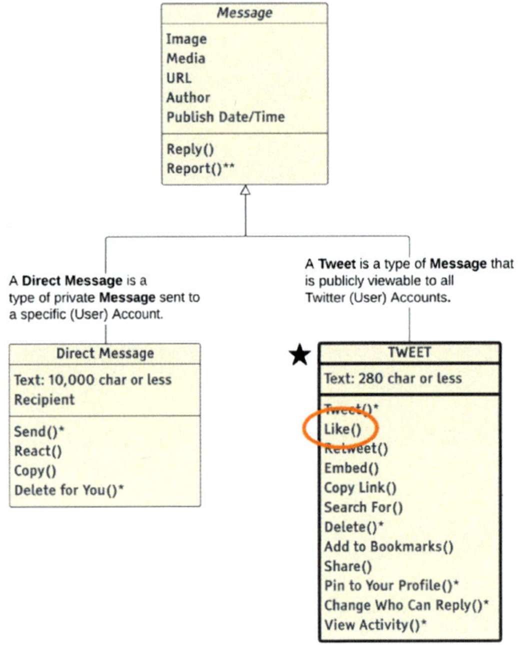

Figure 7.5
The *Like* action is available for a *Tweet* but not a *Direct Message*.

Creating Page Layouts, Menus, and Button Bars

Chapter 2 covered the central concept of objects and actions and the importance of users understanding what actions are available for each object. We saw the principle of strong object-action associations with the example screens for Twitter (Figure 7.6) and the e-commerce product page (Figure 7.7).

Figure 7.6
Main actions for a tweet clustered in the lower button bar

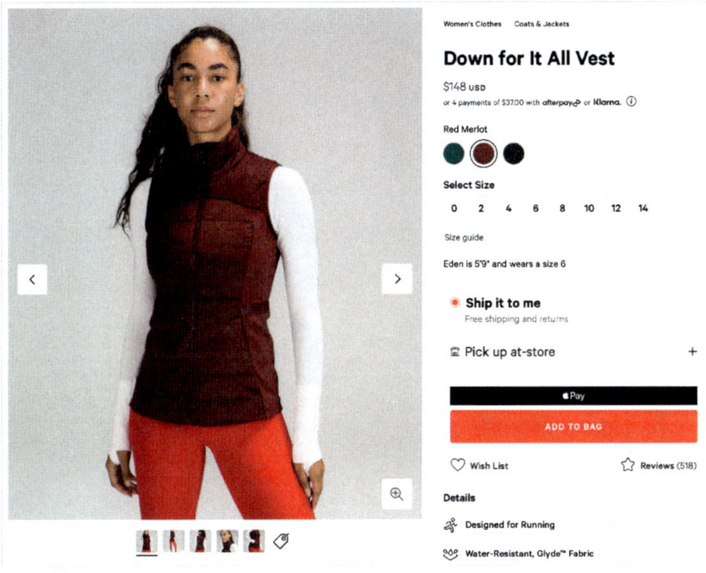

Figure 7.7
Actions for a product consolidated to the right on the product image

An object model is ideal for ensuring that all actions are appropriately present and surfaced in page layouts, menus, and button bars. Imagine if we were building Twitter from scratch, we could use the Tweet object in the model, and all the objects related to it, to start building the experience.

However, keep in mind that the object model represents just one perspective: the structural perspective. Ultimately design should be driven by the task perspective:

how users want to perform tasks, the relative priority of the tasks, and the frequency with which the tasks are performed. Figures 7.6 and 7.7 show a clear hierarchy of actions with the highest priority actions getting the most prominence in the interface. The task perspective necessarily informs their designs. The object model, therefore, is always a complement to (not a replacement for) task-perspective artifacts such as user research findings, journey maps, and task flows.

The complementary nature of the object model is why I decided to pair the discussion of object modeling with how to effectively capture task flows, the topic covered in the next chapter. This book's final chapter, "Real-World Structure and Flow," covers how these two perspectives work together in the design process.

"An object model provides a concise, compact view of a system. If you created the model as a team, you have the benefit of having a shared understanding of the system."

Chapter 08

Capturing Task Flows

The structural perspective, which we explored through object modeling, lays the foundation for the user experience. But design is fundamentally about creating task flows that support people accomplishing their goals. Effective design results from synthesizing both the structural and task perspectives (Figure 8.1).

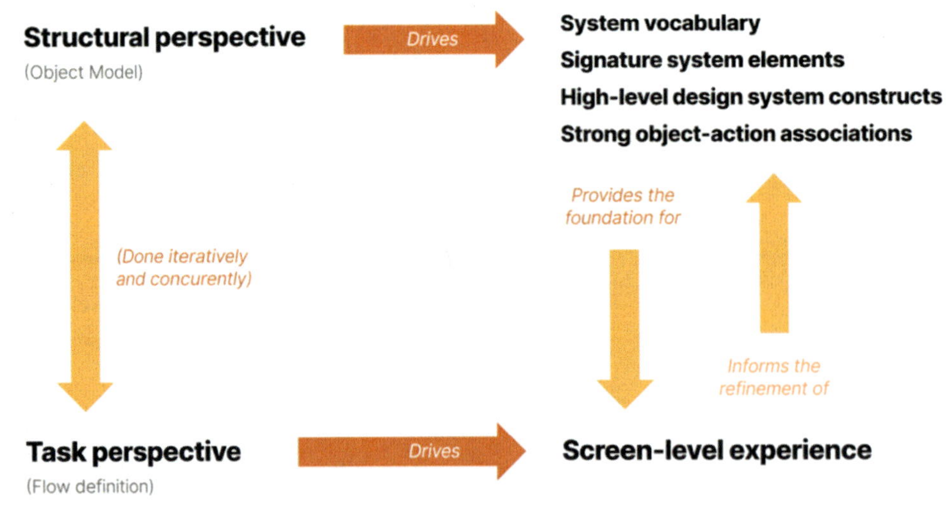

Figure 8.1
The dual perspectives of structure and flow

Representing Task Flows

Task flows are central to a user experience. Consumers experience task flows when they purchase a product, create a social media post, or add a song to a playlist. In the enterprise, task flows may be as simple as updating a loan application or as complex as responding to a power outage. The simplest task flows may have only a single path to success. More complex flows have multiple success paths driven by either user choices or underlying system logic.

There are three main ways to represent task flows:

- Diagrammatically, using flowcharting symbols or rough screen illustrations
- Narratively, such as with written scenarios, storyboards, and use cases
- Interactively, with a prototype that presents each screen one at a time, demonstrating the task flow through that sequence

Figure 8.2 plots common task flow artifacts according to their form and level of granularity.

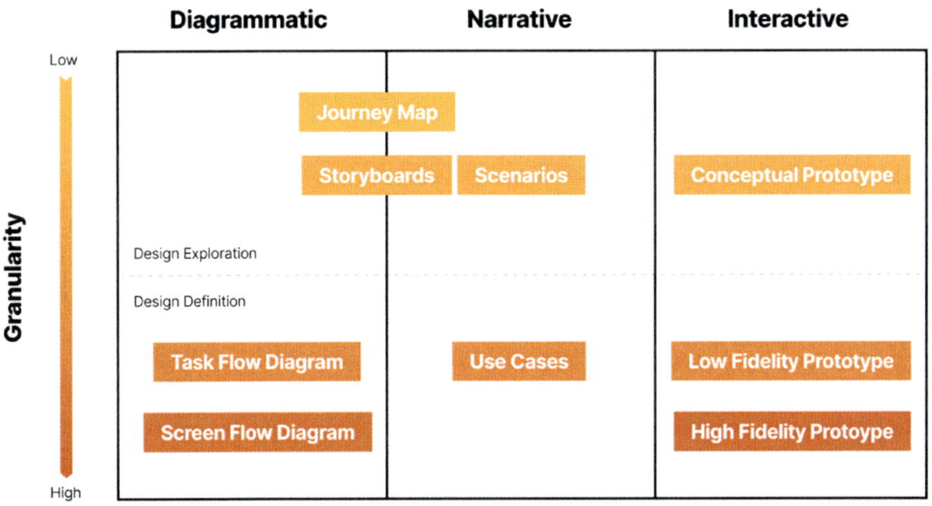

Figure 8.2
Common task flow artifacts

Beyond Prototyping

Designers are likely to be most familiar and comfortable representing flows in a prototype; indeed, today's design tools make it quick and easy to "wire together" individual screens into an interactive prototype. Prototypes can be crucial artifacts for evaluating the design and communicating the design intent for development. However, creating a prototype is not always enough to ensure a good design outcome.

In creating a prototype, designers often focus on a single success path. In this case, the design may not adequately address alternative paths, and it may require refactoring once it gets into development. In this situation, developers (who vary in UX skills and ability to propose effective design solutions) often handle the needed re-work. What results may not represent the best experience for users.

In sum, a prototype is an essential part of the hand-off as it demonstrates key elements. But it usually does not convey the whole design story.

Given the abundant resources available elsewhere, we will not revisit prototyping methods here. Instead, we will focus on diagrammatic and narrative representations of flows that designers may overlook as unfamiliar or something another role, such as a business analyst, might produce. The reality is that another role might not be available to work out the logic around flows. Additionally, designers can easily do this work in a lightweight manner that improves design outcomes and saves time in development.

Key Task Flow Artifacts

The sections that follow cover three primary artifacts used to define task flows:

- Task Flow Diagrams
- Use Cases
- Screen Flow Diagrams

As shown in Figure 8.3, these artifacts are intended for design definition and may be informed by earlier, more exploratory representations of task flows such as journey maps and storyboards.

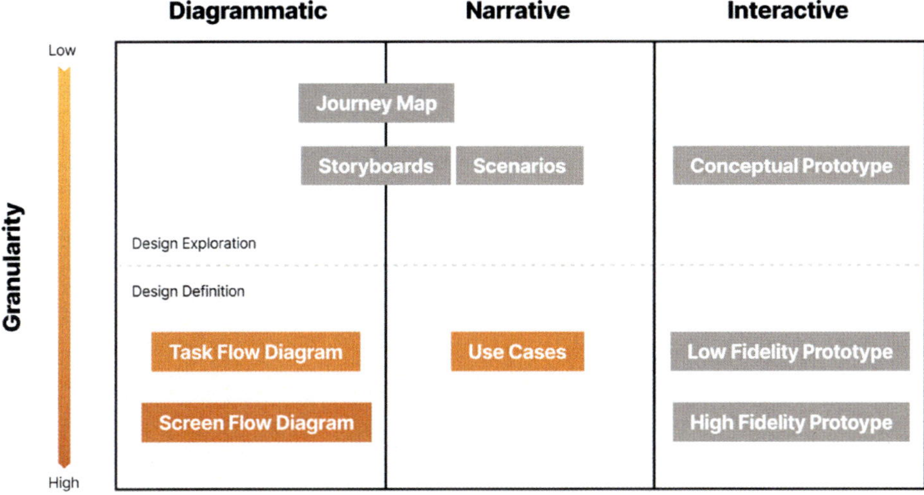

Figure 8.3
Key task flow artifacts: the task flow diagram, screen flow diagram, and use cases

Main versus Alternative Task Flows

Flow diagrams and use cases share the important ability to capture alternative task flows: different paths to a successful outcome that a system must support as part of the user experience. There are two main drivers of alternative flows:

- Pre-conditions
- Choices the user makes

Pre-Conditions

Pre-conditions are the situations existing at the start of a task flow that determine the flow's path. A simple pre-condition for a purchase flow is whether the user is logged in to an existing account. Users who are logged in have one purchase path; users who are not logged in have another (guest checkout).

Pre-conditions can drive significant branches in a business process. In a system used to manage power distribution, there were two pre-conditions: either the equipment in the field was instrumented for remote re-routing of power or it was not. This pre-condition (instrumented or not) set up two potential paths when responding to a power outage:

- Where remote switching is available (the primary path), power can be re-routed from the operations center.
- When remote switching is unavailable (the alternative path), the engineer must dispatch a field crew to re-route the power on-site.

Thinking through the possible pre-conditions for a task is a great starting point for identifying alternative paths.

Choices the User Makes

Alternative paths also result from choices the user makes. For example:

- When placing an order on an e-commerce site, users may have "Pay Now" options such as Apple Pay and PayPal, as well as a more traditional cart checkout option that requires more steps. Each payment method has a different path to completion.
- When a user signs up for a new service, the different paths available could depend on the type of account the user selects (such as enterprise, small business, or personal).

Depicting Alternative Paths

We will look at two methods of depicting alternative flows: flow diagrams and use cases. Flow diagrams have the advantage of visually indicating the point at which an alternative path begins, and what upstream conditions or actions are driving that path. In many situations, a flow diagram will suffice. However, the design intent of complex workflows can sometimes be more clearly described in a narrative (with a use case).

Creating Flow Diagrams

If you aren't already familiar with standard flow diagramming symbols, using them can give your diagramming efforts a real boost. Adhering to the standard conventions makes it easier to create diagrams, and your diagrams will be easier for others to consume.

Flow diagrams began being used in the 1920s to document business processes. In the 1940s, as the practice of flow diagramming widened, the conventions were formalized by the American Society of Mechanical Engineers (ASME). By the late 1940s, flow diagrams were increasingly used in the developing field of computer programming.

Figure 8.4 shows four must-know symbols for flow diagramming:

- The rectangle, indicating a process
- The diamond, indicating a decision
- The rounded rectangle (terminator), which shows where the process ends
- The off-page reference, which allows you to link to another related task flow diagram

Figure 8.4 also shows a fifth symbol — an oval, indicating user actions that initiate or commit a function. This symbol is handy in UX flow diagrams to highlight the major user actions, as we'll see in the examples that follow.

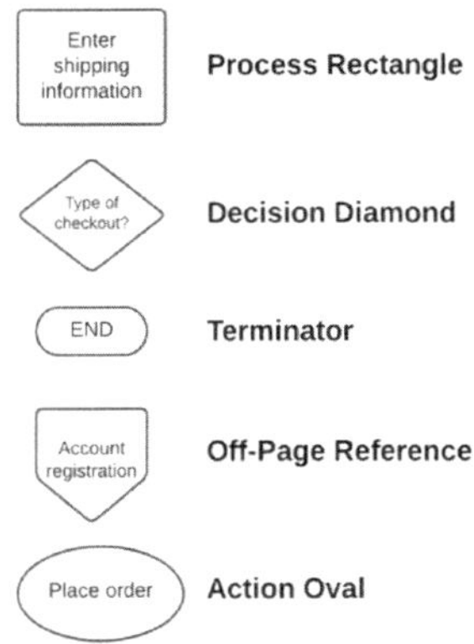

Figure 8.4
Key flow diagramming symbols for UX

Figure 8.5 uses the above symbols to illustrate a checkout flow for an e-commerce site.

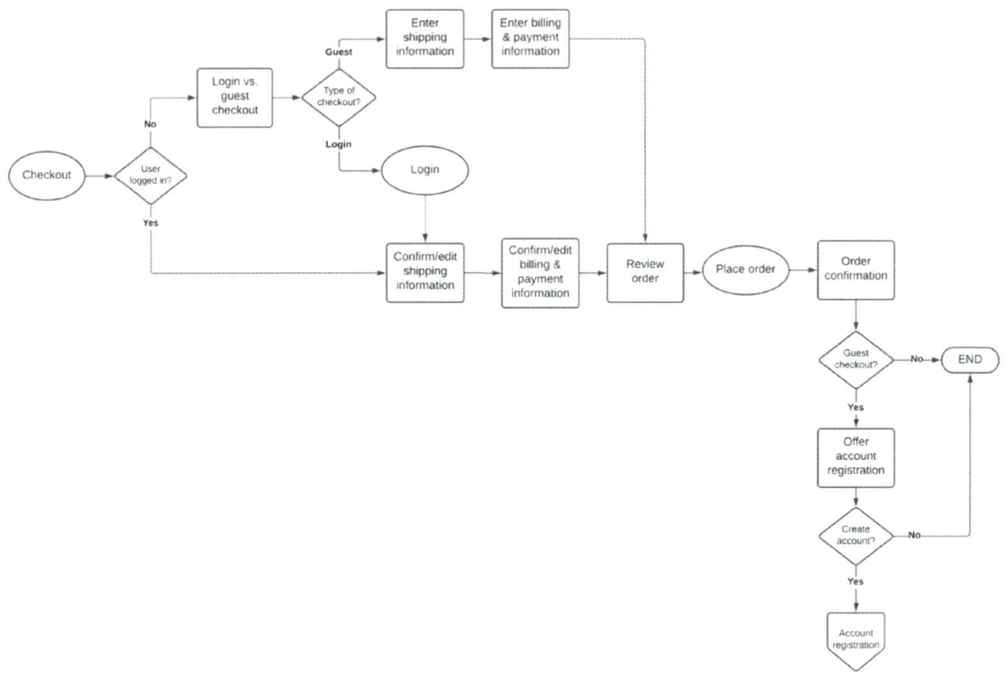

Figure 8.5
Checkout task flow for an e-commerce site. You can also view this diagram at objectmodelingfordesigners.com/chapter-8

Figure 8.5 is an example of a **task flow diagram**. Each rectangle describes a step in the process, but the screen-level experience is not yet defined. Each step might represent one or possibly more screens. As the design progresses, the task flow diagram can evolve into a **screen flow diagram**, which depicts the actual screens the user will experience as part of the flow.

The Decision Diamond

The decision diamond is the key to representing alternative paths; it illustrates branches in the flow and what conditions or actions drive each branch. Usually, the decision diamond contains a yes/no question so that there is a yes branch and a no branch.

Figure 8.6 is a task flow for re-routing power in response to an outage. The user (a power distribution engineer) initiates the flow by opening a new ticket. There are two possible pre-conditions: either the equipment is instrumented for remote switching or not. These pre-conditions drive a branch in the flow, represented by the yes/no question "Remote switching possible?" in the decision diamond.

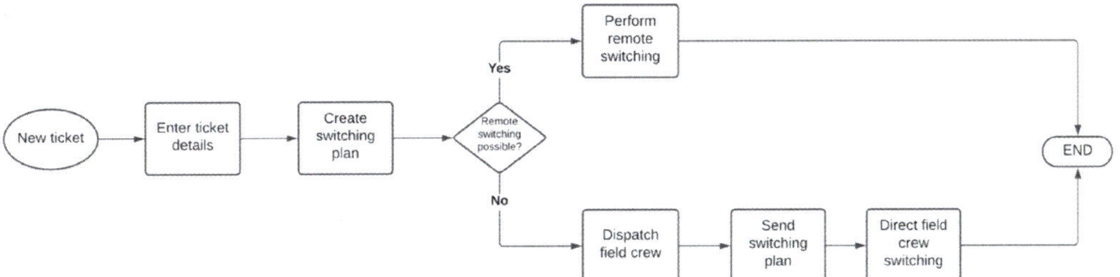

Figure 8.6
Task flow for re-routing power. You can also view this diagram at objectmodelingfordesigners.com/chapter-8

The decision diamond can also represent explicit selections available to the user, as shown in Figure 8.7. Here, the decision diamond represents a data field (account type), and the branches represent the possible selected values (enterprise, small business, personal).

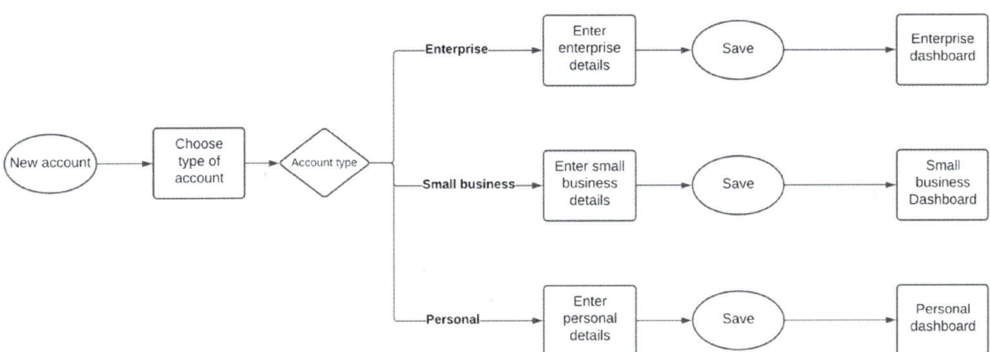

Figure 8.7
Branch of a task flow based on data selection (account type). You can also view this diagram at objectmodelingfordesigners.com/chapter-8

Using Line Labeling to Show System Response

Figure 8.8 is a smaller-scale flow for creating a new risk in a risk management system. The diagram shows how to use line labeling to indicate the system's response to a user action:

- If the user saves the risk as a draft, the system adds it to the "Drafts" list.
- If the user publishes the risk, the system adds it to the "Recently Created" list.

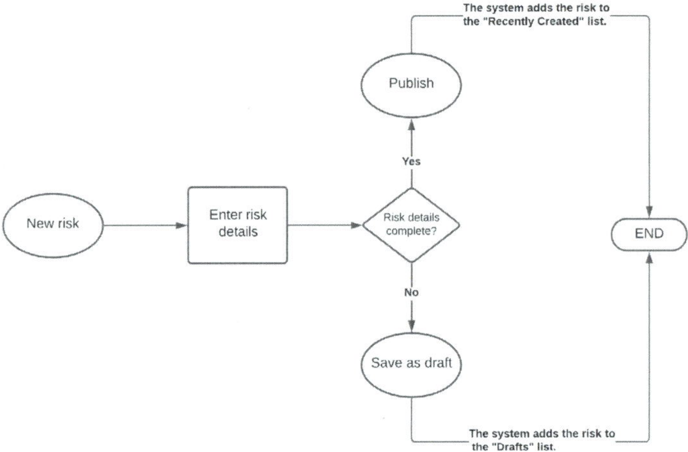

Figure 8.8
Task flow showing the system response in a line label. You can also view this diagram at objectmodelingfordesigners.com/chapter-8

It's not always necessary to include the system response to a user action (in most cases, it's self-evident). Still, it can be helpful in some situations to clarify system functionality.

Swim Lanes

You may need to illustrate task flows that progress across more than one role, particularly with more complex systems. In this case, you can create a swim lane for each role. Figure 8.9, a task flow diagram for re-routing power, shows all three roles involved in the process: Quality Assurance, Distribution Engineer, and Field Crew.

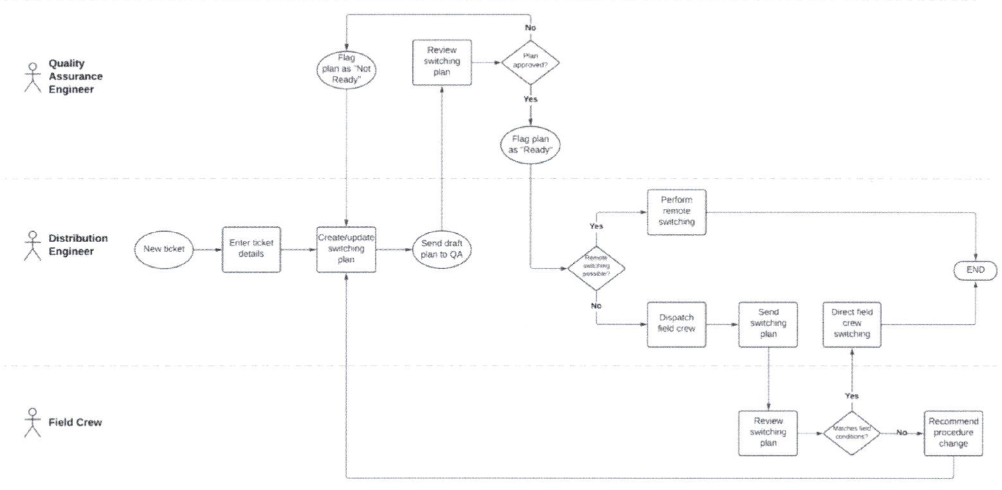

Figure 8.9
Task flow diagram with swim lanes. You can also view this diagram at objectmodelingfordesigners.com/chapter-8

The advantage of showing task flows across all roles involved in a process is that it allows you to see the entire process, including the interaction between roles, which can be an essential consideration when designing more complex systems.

Use Case Narratives

In the previous section, we saw how task flow diagrams illustrate flows visually. This section will cover how to capture flows in the narrative as **use cases**.

There is sometimes confusion about the difference between user stories and use cases. I have seen some designers equate the two or position user stories as a more modern, "evolved" version of a use case. However, user stories and use cases are not equivalent artifacts:

- User stories describe tasks in terms of result and benefit and are written mainly from the business perspective. In Agile development, user stories are intended to generate discussion and are therefore intentionally brief. In previous chapters, we worked with example user stories for Twitter, an e-commerce system, and Slack.
- A use case is more detailed and definitive: it describes the user's sequence of interactions with the system to achieve a goal. A use case's purpose is to guide design and development.

With the advent of Agile development, fully developed use case narratives have somewhat fallen out of favor. However, use cases can be a powerful tool that ensures that a design covers all the needed situations, particularly in more complex flows. Understanding the use case format gives you another tool in your toolkit.

Use case narratives follow a prescribed outline, specifying actors, pre-conditions, primary ("happy day") flows, alternative flows, and exception flows. Like task flow diagrams, they describe **what** should happen but not **how**. I've found that verbalizing a flow in a use case narrative can help generate additional ideas about the primary flow and needed alternative flows. I like to think of use cases as a highly evolved (and more structured) storyboard narrative.

The Use Case Outline

As a starting point, it's helpful to outline a use case. Even if you don't go all-in on writing use cases, writing a use case outline can be a helpful exercise, and you can use it to provide additional context for a task flow diagram.

The use case outline has these elements:

- The **Overview** summarizes the purpose of the use case.
- The **Actor** represents the user type or role.
- **Pre-Conditions** are situations that must be true for the flow to occur.
- The **Primary (Happy Day) Flow** is the flow under ideal conditions.
- **Alternative Flows** represent the flow under alternative conditions.
- **Exceptions** are conditions or actions that result in users not achieving use case's goal.

Below is an example use case outline for cart checkout.

Use Case: Cart Checkout
Overview: Cart checkout is method customers can use to place an order
Actor: Customer
Pre-Conditions: The user has at least one item in the cart
Primary (Happy Day) Flow: The user is logged into their account
Alternative Flow A: The user is not logged into an account (guest checkout)
Exceptions: At any point up to placing the order, the user may cancel the checkout

In this example, it may seem unnecessary to state that there must be at least one item in the cart, but explicitly thinking about pre-conditions can help avoid making wrong assumptions about the circumstances for a flow. We also have additional pre-condition statements for the primary and alternative flows. These statements define the specific conditions governing those flows.

Figure 8.10 shows how a use case outline and a task flow diagram can work together.

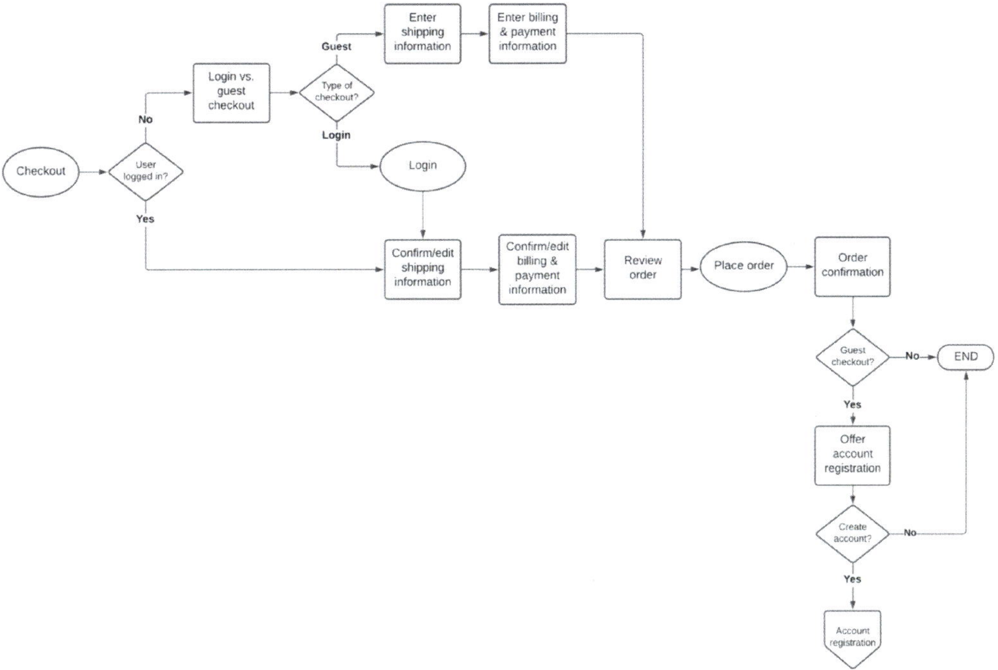

Figure 8.10
Task flow diagram with a use case outline. You can also view this diagram at objectmodelingfordesigners.com/chapter-8

The Full Use Case Narrative

A complete use case describes the primary and alternative flows in a narrative format, typically as a set of actions between the user and the system (as shown in the cart checkout example below).

Example Use Case Narrative

Use Case: Cart Checkout
Overview: Cart checkout is method customers can use to place an order
Actor: Customer
Pre-conditions: The user has at least one item in the cart

Primary (Happy Day) Flow: The user is logged into their account.

1) The user initiates "Check Out."
2) The user confirms their shipping information. If needed, they may edit the information.
3) The user confirms their billing and payment information. If needed, they may edit the information.
4) The user reviews the order information and submits the order.
5) The system displays an order confirmation.

Alternative Flow A: The user is not logged into an account (guest checkout).
If the user is checking out as a guest, the user enters, rather than confirms, shipping, billing, and payment information.

Exceptions: At any point up to placing the order, the user may cancel the checkout.

The example above is designed to illustrate the format; the simplicity of these steps wouldn't otherwise warrant writing them out in narrative. I could have easily captured the steps in a task flow diagram or, as we'll see in a later section, directly as a screen flow diagram.

Consider, however, writing a use case narrative when there are business rules that are more clearly expressed verbally. In Exercise F, you'll use a use case narrative containing more descriptive steps.

Use Cases: Q & A

Below are some common questions that come up when I talk about use cases.

Q: What is the relationship between a task flow diagram and a use case narrative?

A: Task flow diagrams and use case narratives are roughly equivalent artifacts: both define primary and alternative flows and describe what happens in a flow, not how it happens at the screen level. As we saw with the e-commerce checkout example, there is no need to write a complete narrative for simpler flows. However, a use case narrative provides more flexibility to add information and context around each step—an option that can be helpful when defining more complex flows.

Q: What is the relationship between user stories and use cases?

A: User stories and use cases were developed within two different development methodologies (Agile Software Development and Rational Unified Process, respectively). As such, they don't have a formalized, methodology-based relationship. However, a use case generally expands upon and further defines a user story statement.

Q: What is a use case diagram?

A: A use case diagram visually represents all use cases associated with a system. The use case diagram's conventions are part of the Unified Modeling Language (UML). Each oval in the diagram represents a use case; lines show the relationships between use cases and between use cases and actors (users). Figure 8.11 is a use case model for an e-commerce system.

Figure 8.11
Use case diagram for an e-commerce system. You can also view this diagram at objectmodelingfordesigners.com/chapter-8

As a designer, I think it's worth knowing what a use case diagram is, but I don't see a use for them in today's design practice. In my experience, use case diagrams can quickly get visually complex and are challenging for stakeholders to understand.

Q: Do use case narratives really have a place in today's Agile world?

A: Authoring use cases takes time and thought, but writing even rough narratives can be a huge time-saver downstream where requirements might otherwise be unclear. The narratives provide a structure for thinking about pre-conditions, primary and alternative flows, and situations where the use case's goal cannot be achieved (exceptions).

For complex systems, I selectively provide use case narratives as part of the development hand-off. Developers receiving the narratives have always appreciated the level of clarity that they provide.

Exercise F: Flow Diagramming

Using standard flow diagramming symbols (as shown in Figure 8.4), create a flow diagram from the following use case for a ride-hailing service. The solution is in the next section.

Use Case Narrative

Use Case: Request and Complete a Trip
Overview: How a passenger gets to their desired destination
Actor: Passenger
Pre-conditions: The passenger has registered for an account with the service.

Primary (Happy Day) Flow: User accepts and takes the trip.

1) The passenger opens the mobile app.
2) The system displays a map showing the passenger's location and an estimated pickup time based on drivers in the area.
3) The passenger selects "Get Ride."
4) The system asks the passenger to review their pickup location to ensure it's correct. If it's not correct, they have the option to enter their location manually.
5) The passenger confirms the pickup location.
6) The passenger enters the desired destination location.
7) The system displays the trip's estimated time and cost.
8) The passenger reviews the time and cost and finalizes their trip request. In response, a driver accepts the trip.
9) The system displays information about the driver who accepted the trip, including the estimated pickup time. The map shows the driver's progress toward the pickup.
10) The driver picks up the passenger; the map shows the driver's progress to the destination, including the estimated arrival time.
11) The passenger arrives at the destination; the system indicates the trip has concluded and offers the option to leave a tip for the driver.

Exception A: Before finalizing their trip request, the passenger finds the estimated time or cost of the trip unacceptable. In this case, the passenger may cancel out of the flow.
Exception B: The passenger wants to cancel the trip after requesting it but before

the driver arrives. In this case, the passenger can cancel the trip; there is no charge if they cancel within 5 minutes of the driver accepting the trip. If they cancel later than that, they are charged a cancellation fee.

Exercise F: Solution

In Exercise F, you created a task flow diagram for the use case **Request and Complete a Trip**. The example solution is below (Figure 8.12):

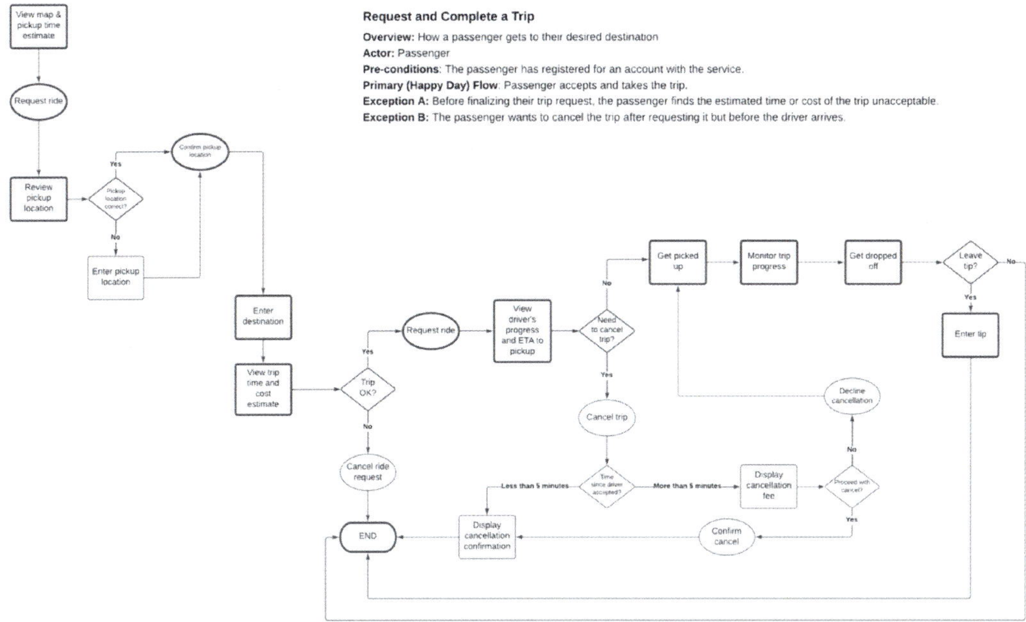

Figure 8.12

Task flow diagram for Request and Complete a Trip. You can also view this diagram at objectmodelingfordesigners.com/chapter-8

About the Solution

I built the diagram by first creating the primary path (using symbols that have a bold outline). Next, I reviewed the exception paths, adding the needed symbols and using a normal-weight outline to distinguish them from the main path. Note how the decision diamonds help communicate the conditions driving branches in the finished diagram (Figure 8.12).

Screen Flow Diagrams

A task flow diagram can, as the design progresses, evolve into a screen flow diagram. A screen flow diagram illustrates how the flow will be implemented from a design standpoint. Figure 8.13 shows a screen flow diagram for the task flow in Exercise F (request and complete a trip for a ride-hailing service).

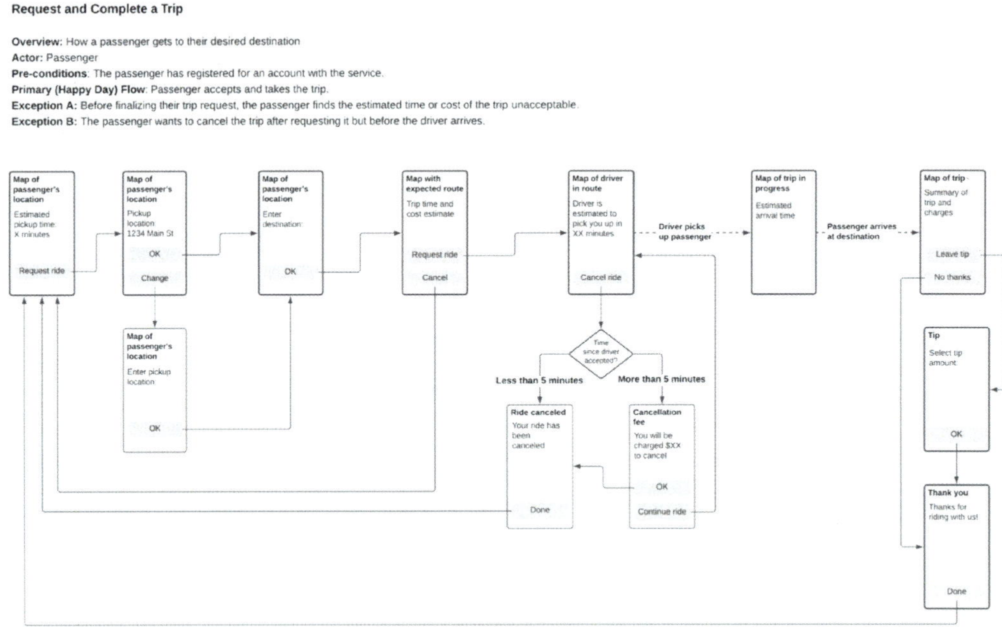

Figure 8.13

Screen flow diagram for Request and Complete a Trip. You can also view this diagram at objectmodelingfordesigners.com/chapter-8

Figure 8.13 (above) uses **screen schematics**—a high-level form of wireframe—to illustrate the flow. Each screen schematic represents a screen or a specific state of a screen. Figure 8.14 shows the format in more detail:

- The screen name or description is in the upper left, in bold text.
- A representation of screen content is in the center.
- Buttons that move the user forward or backward in the flow are at the bottom of the schematic. Lines connecting each button to its destination screen or screen state illustrate the movement of the flow.

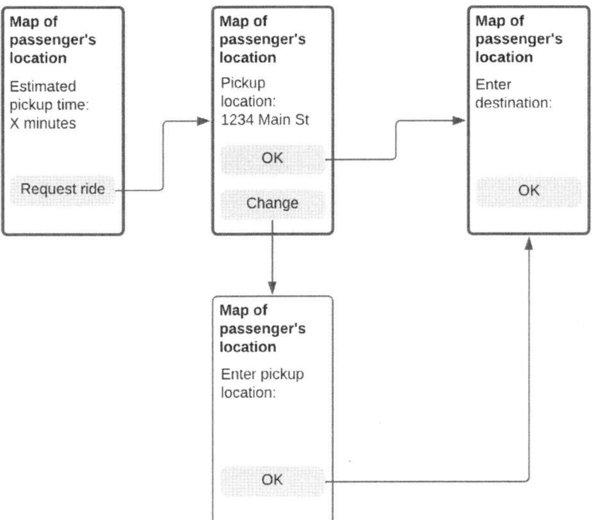

Figure 8.14
Screen flow diagram detail

Note that there are many different styles of screen flow diagrams, and they can be done at varying levels of visual fidelity (including final screen thumbnails). The screen schematics shown here are intended to come before screen-level design; they illustrate key elements on each page and how they advance the flow (or otherwise function). Other screen details, such as global navigation, are omitted in this case. Feel free, of course, to adapt the format to fit your particular design situation.

System-Generated Flow

A task flow diagram represents the general steps needed to complete a flow. Because a screen flow diagram illustrates the user experience in more detail, it may also need to depict actions the system takes. Figure 8.15 is an example of the system automatically advancing the flow (minus any needed interaction by the user). It shows how the screen state automatically changes once the passenger enters the driver's car and begins their trip, and changes again when they arrive at their destination. A dashed line between the screen states indicates this system-driven advancement.

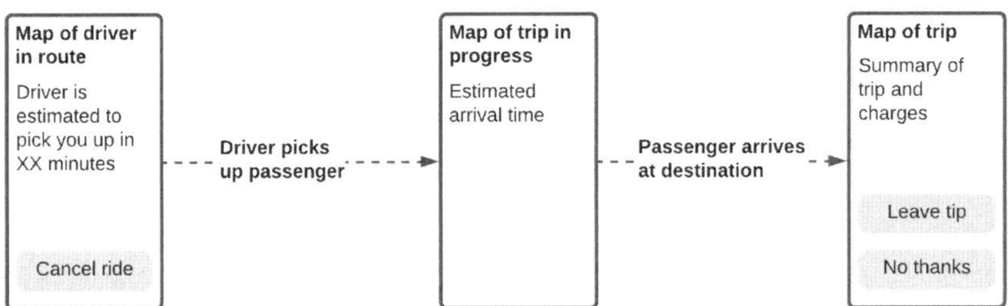

Figure 8.15
The system advancing the flow based on the user's location

Branching the Flow

In a screen flow diagram, buttons represent user actions that advance the flow and drive branches in the flow (as shown in Figure 8.16).

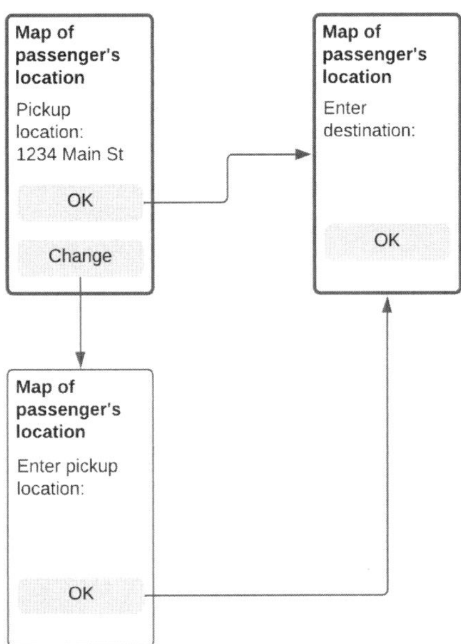

Figure 8.16
A branch in the flow driven by a user-selected option

However, there may also be branching driven by system logic—for example, whether it's been more than five minutes since the driver accepted the ride. In this case, the decision diamond illustrates the branch (as shown in Figure 8.17).

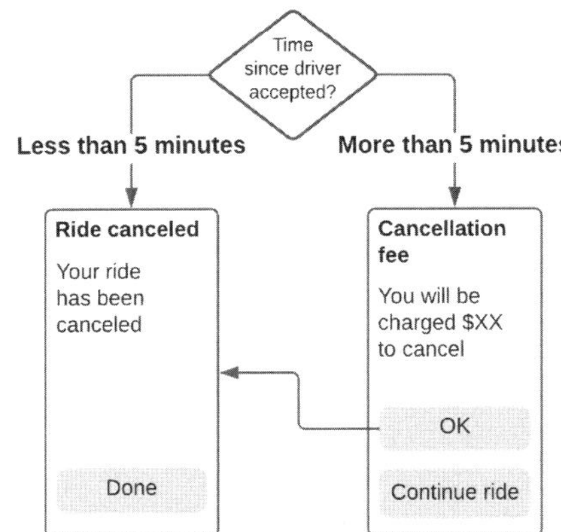

Figure 8.17
A branch in the flow driven by system logic

Exercise G: Creating a Screen Flow Diagram

For your final exercise, you'll use Figure 8.18, the task flow diagram for an e-commerce checkout, to create a screen flow diagram. An example solution is in the next section.

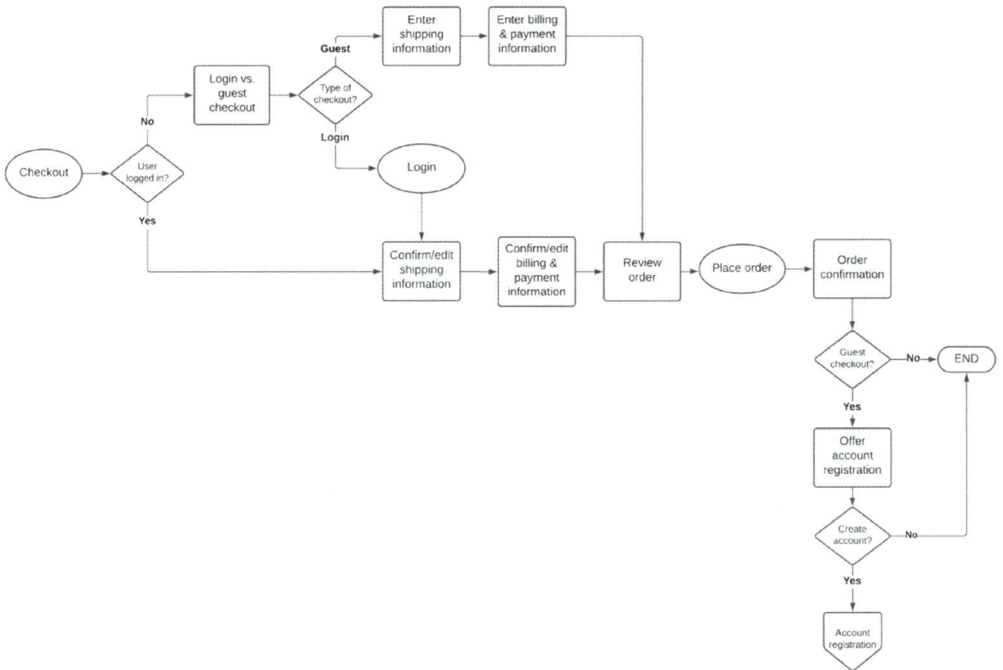

Figure 8.18

Task flow diagram for e-commerce checkout. You can also view this diagram at objectmodelingfordesigners.com/chapter-8

Exercise G Solution

In Exercise G, you used a task flow diagram to create a screen flow diagram. Figure 8.19 shows the example solution.

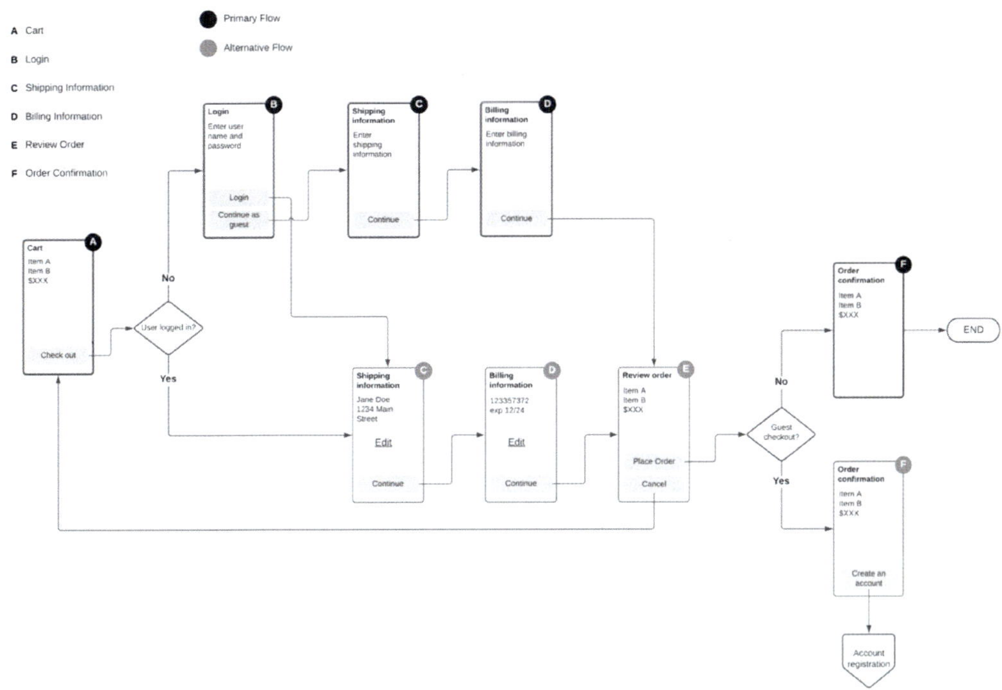

Figure 8.19

Screen flow diagram for e-commerce checkout. You can also view this diagram at objectmodelingfordesigners.com/chapter-8

About the Solution

I've used a couple of elements in this screen flow diagram to show additional presentation options. With this flow, some of the same screens (Shipping Information and Billing Information) are shown in different states (driven by whether the user is logged in). To help highlight the multiple instances of those screens, I assigned a letter key to each discrete page type. Additionally, I used a black annotation marker for screens in the primary flow and a gray annotation marker for screens in the alternative flow.

Tips for Capturing Flows

As with object modeling, consider flow diagramming and use case narratives as tools in your designer's toolkit. Deploy these tools where flows require further clarification and definition. The tips below should help you get started.

Make Flow Definition an Integral Part of the Design Process

Task flow diagramming or writing use case narratives can help you think through the needed paths and factors driving those paths. I've sometimes seen designers create flow diagrams at the very end of a design process—as part of the development hand-off—long after the entire experience is "baked." This approach represents a missed opportunity to use flow diagramming or narratives as part of the design process to create a better, more thoughtful experience.

Start with the Primary Flow

Particularly for more complex flows, identifying all the possible branches and factors driving the branches can feel daunting. Start with the primary (happy day) flow, and then work out the alternative flows, understanding that how you construct the primary flow may change as you work out the alternatives.

Double-Check Your Work

Flow diagrams must not have logic flaws or dead-end paths, so be sure to double-check your work or, better yet, walk through it with a colleague. Explaining the flow and logic to others often highlights problems that you wouldn't otherwise identify.

Choose the Fidelity of Flow Diagram That Best Suits Your Need

This chapter covered two types of flow diagrams—the task flow diagram and the screen flow diagram. In some cases, it makes sense to prepare both, particularly when requirements are unclear. However, you may find that you can work directly with a screen flow diagram for more straightforward flows or updates to existing flows.

Get Creative with Flow Diagramming

Flow diagrams are intended to communicate, so anything you can do to enhance their clarity is a plus. Feel free to extend or otherwise adapt the basic conventions presented here. However, remember that using standard symbols will make your diagrams easier for others to read and understand.

Flow Diagramming Quick Reference

The quick reference guide below may also be viewed or downloaded at objectmodelingfordesigners.com/resources

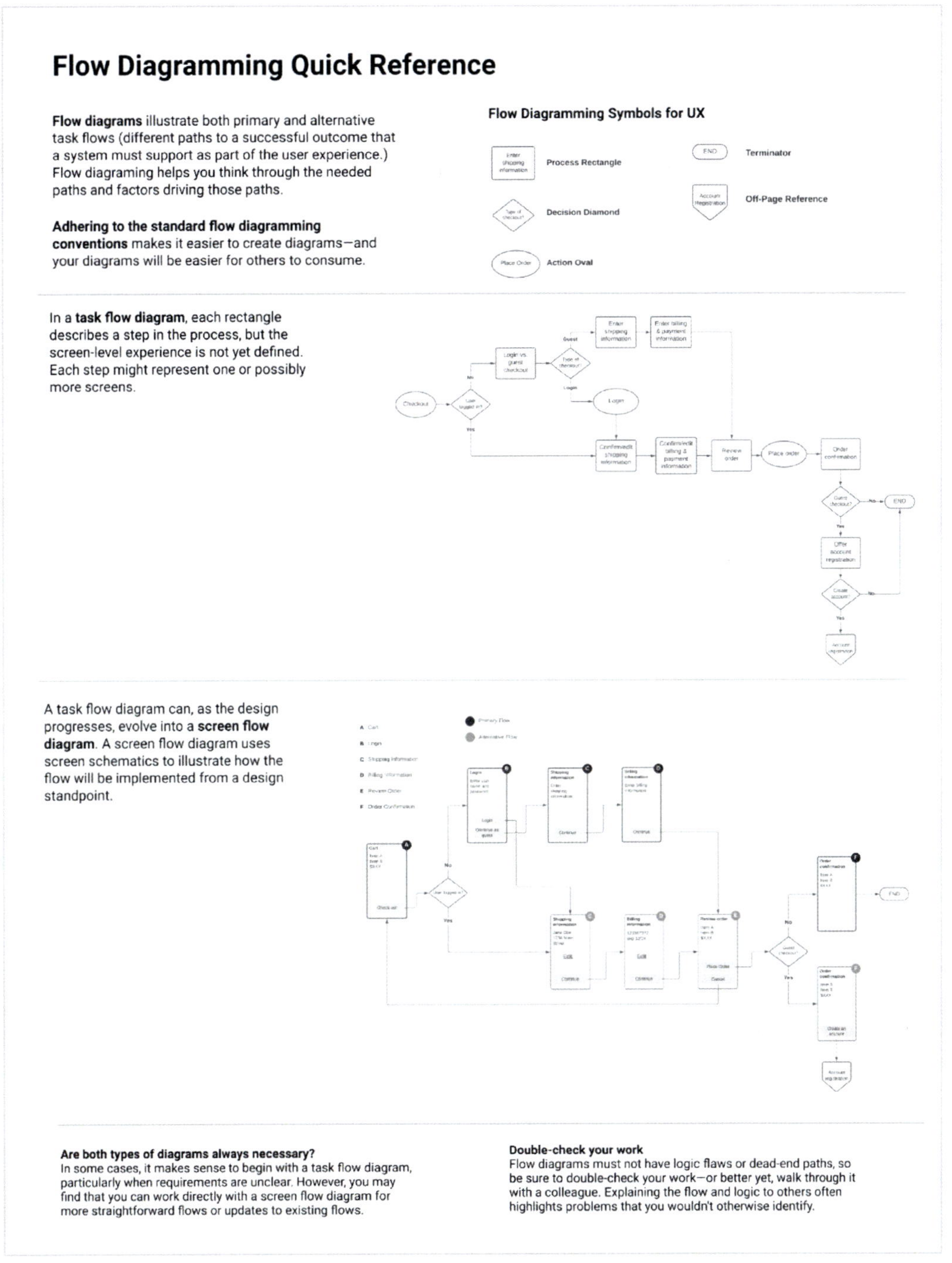

Flow Diagramming Quick Reference

Flow diagrams illustrate both primary and alternative task flows (different paths to a successful outcome that a system must support as part of the user experience.) Flow diagraming helps you think through the needed paths and factors driving those paths.

Adhering to the standard flow diagramming conventions makes it easier to create diagrams—and your diagrams will be easier for others to consume.

Flow Diagramming Symbols for UX

In a **task flow diagram**, each rectangle describes a step in the process, but the screen-level experience is not yet defined. Each step might represent one or possibly more screens.

A task flow diagram can, as the design progresses, evolve into a **screen flow diagram**. A screen flow diagram uses screen schematics to illustrate how the flow will be implemented from a design standpoint.

Are both types of diagrams always necessary?
In some cases, it makes sense to begin with a task flow diagram, particularly when requirements are unclear. However, you may find that you can work directly with a screen flow diagram for more straightforward flows or updates to existing flows.

Double-check your work
Flow diagrams must not have logic flaws or dead-end paths, so be sure to double-check your work—or better yet, walk through it with a colleague. Explaining the flow and logic to others often highlights problems that you wouldn't otherwise identify.

Chapter 09

Real-World Structure and Flow

If there's anything I've learned in my consulting career, it's that there is no one-size-fits-all design process. Design is a highly situational endeavor. The approach depends on the overall business context, the design problems that need solving, and the project team dynamic. So how does developing an object model and capturing flows fit into real-world design efforts?

Emphasis on Structure versus Flow

Separate sections of this book cover the structural perspective (building an object model) and the task perspective (capturing task flows). In real-world design, the perspectives of structure and flow are complementary and should be developed concurrently (Figure 9.1).

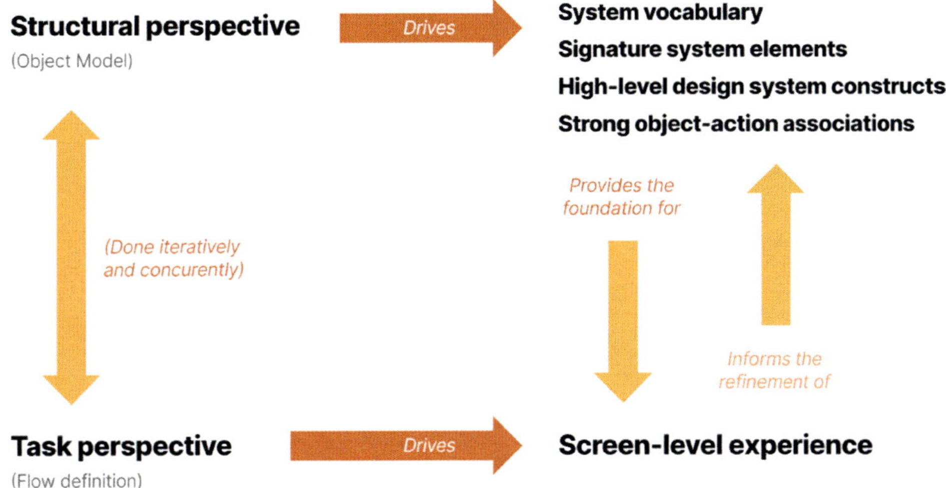

Figure 9.1
The dual perspectives of structure and flow

Early design explorations are necessarily flow-oriented since that perspective mirrors how users interact with a system. Journey maps, storyboards, scenarios, conceptual prototypes all serve as the basis for building an experience. You can identify key objects, object relationships, and actions from these early artifacts and capture them in a preliminary model. An early object model can inform design explorations, and design explorations, in turn, inform the object model.

The object model serves as the basis of a consistent, cohesive foundation for the experience, including the system's architecture, vocabulary, and design conventions. The model helps designers make strong associations between objects and its actions at the screen level, associations that are critical to system usability.

Capturing task flows in diagrams or narratives helps ensure a design will meet users' needs across all situations and that the design supports both the primary flow and all needed alternative flows, not just the primary flow.

All design projects have some element of defining structure and flow. However, depending upon the situation, there can be more or less emphasis on the structural perspective. In general:

- More structural definition is required for greenfield design and complete system redesigns.
- Less structural definition is needed for incremental releases, which normally must fit existing structural conventions.

Working within Agile Development Methods

Agile methods arose in the early 2000s as a reaction against the waterfall methods that prevailed at the time. In waterfall, the entire system, including its design, is defined up-front before any development work begins. Particularly with large systems, vast amounts of time and effort can go into producing requirements documentation. As a result, there is a long history of waterfall methods creating systems that were already "legacy" at launch because business needs had shifted by the time development was completed. To avoid this fate, Agile prescribes building working code in two or three-week sprints. Conversations between team members essentially replace formal requirements documentation.

Today, most organizations profess to use Agile methods rather than waterfall. You might ask, therefore, how the artifacts described in this book fit with Agile.

Despite its popularity, Agile comes with its own set of shortcomings, and most organizations' Agile aspirations rarely match the reality of how development work gets done. In my experience, organizations have difficulty practicing "pure" Agile because it runs counter to the human instinct to plan work before performing it. In more mature organizations, waterfall methods are often entrenched and persist despite Agile-looking project plans. I've still found developers (sometimes clandestinely) producing formal requirements documentation, including UML class diagrams, even in younger companies with no organizational history using waterfall.

In short, there are usually opportunities, even in the context of Agile development, to model a system's structure and flow. Today's Agile processes usually incorporate user-centered design practices, with provisions for UX work to run in advance of the development sprints. The configuration of sprints will govern the timing and pacing of object modeling and flow diagramming that you do. Even where a sprint structure lacks formal support for design planning, you may still find informal support for your efforts among developers, who, in my experience, welcome definition and clarity that makes their jobs easier.

Keeping It Light and Adaptive

My final piece of advice is to make sure you keep any object models or flow diagrams as light as possible, providing just enough detail to meet the circumstance. Avoid the temptation with object modeling in particular to needlessly perfect the model.

I also invite you to adapt and refine the methods presented in this book. I intend to inspire, not legislate. Every design circumstance has its unique challenges and requirements. Feel free to use these methods to meet those challenges in the way that you think fits best.

Resources and References

Resources

Object modeling for designers. https://www.objectmodelingfordesigners.com/

This book's website contains all models, diagrams, quick reference materials, and additional resources. Diagrams from the book are specifically located at objectmodelingfordesigners.com/book

Lucidchart. https://www.lucidchart.com/
Models and diagrams for this book were created using Lucidchart.

References

Collins, D. (1995). Designing object-oriented user interfaces. Benjamin Cummings.

Connolly, E. The Full Stack Design System. https://www.intercom.com/blog/the-full-stack-design-system/

Harmelen, M. V. (2001). *Object modeling and user interface design*. Addison-Wesley.

Mall, D. Distinct Design Systems https://superfriendly.com/design-systems/articles/distinct-design-systems/

Made in the USA
Coppell, TX
05 January 2023